Beautifully
Unbroken

The Prostitute's Daughter

Jodie Ballenger

New Season Publishing

Fort Wayne, Indiana

New Season Publishing
P.O. Box 25597
Fort Wayne, Indiana 46825
www.jodieballenger.com

Scripture taken from the New King James Version. Copyright 1982 by Thomas Nelson, Inc. Used by permission. All rights reserved.

Statistics - Child Sexual Abuse
www.parentsformeganslaw.org/statistics-child-sexual-abuse/

Beautifully Unbroken/ Jodie Ballenger. -- 1st ed.
ISBN 978-1-7342623-1-5 (Paperback)
ISBN 978-1-7342623-0-8 (Hardcover)

Introduction

The fall season has arrived in Indiana. The brilliant orange and gold leaves on trees signal that winter won't be far behind. I sense the changing of the seasons in my own life as well. The story between the covers of this book has been churning inside for a long while and it is time, the season, to share it in the hope that my life's journey will inspire others to embrace the forgiveness, love and purpose Christ alone provides.

My story is not easy to tell. It conjures up emotions that are not pleasant to remember, but the end message stands as a testimony of God's amazing grace. My childhood and teen years were chaotic, painful and confusing. I had deep-seated anger due to a fragmented, seriously dysfunctional family. I felt the shame of sexual abuse, the sting of abandonment, and a lack of guidance for my life in general. With no spiritual foundation, my reaction to life's unfairness was to become rebellious, promiscuous, and hard.

This is my story as I remember it. My intentions are not to hurt the people in my past but to encourage and give insight to others going through their own personal battles. I also want to bring attention to sexual abuse against children. The statistics are staggering (one in three girls; one in six boys) and probably askew because most cases of sexual abuse against children go unreported. I feel a calling to not only inform but to offer help to these most innocent of victims.

Time will pass and seasons will come and go, but the peace I have found in Christ is ever constant and faithful.

Jodie Ballenger

Fall 2019

This book is dedicated in loving memory of my mom

Judith Arminda Sites: I love and miss you so much. No matter what we went through I always saw the good in you, you were my mom and nothing you did or did not do could change the tremendous love that I have for you. I am so happy that you were in a good place when you left this world. I wish my children could have had more time with you to know how special you were. Your life was full of struggles and hurts from your very first memories. I Pray your story will touch many people. Mom, thank you for being there for me when you could. I am sorry for the times I was not there for you. I LOVE YOU

Instead of being ashamed of what you've been through, be proud of what you have overcome. ~Dr. Phil

My story is filled with broken pieces, terrible choices, and ugly truths. It's also filled with a major comeback, peace in my soul, and grace that saved my Life. ~ Unknown Author

Sometimes the smallest step in the right direction ends up being the biggest step of your life, Tiptoe if you must but take the step. ~ Unknown Author

Guilt tells me I have done something wrong. Shame tells me I am something wrong. ~ Sheila Walsh

We all have chapters we would rather keep unpublished.

~ Downton Abbey

Whether you think you can or think you can't: you're right.

~ Henry Ford

Your past is just a story, and once you realize this, it has no power over you. ~ Unknown Author

If you don't like where you are, move. You're not a tree.

~ Unknown Author

Preface

"Your mom was a prostitute."

The words hung in the air like the smoke from the weed that had been inhaled deep into my lungs. I looked at the woman, her worn, hardscrabble face intently looking at me, and couldn't find a place inside my high to comprehend.

"We used to live together, and she brought men to the house. You look just like her," she said.

I was sixteen and I didn't care. I can still see my mom, my question to her hanging in the air. Her face was filled with anguish, hoping her past could be mended and spackled, the words wanting to bubble out of her mouth. I wanted to shut her down, knowing that whatever she said didn't matter; I didn't want to know the despair she had felt.

I locked eyes with hers. "Mom, they're saying you were a prostitute. Were you?"

She looked straight at me and said, "Yes, I was."

There was no sorrow in her voice and no reaction in mine. I both loved her and rejected her words, I was twisted and tangled in my own destructive years, yet the words I heard from her that day haunt me still.

My mom's name was Judy, and she knew just where hopelessness and despair would take you. Day after day, night after night, she mentally left her body as men took control of it. These lived-through days were full of high danger, where dark streets allowed men to pay for the only thing she had to offer. She put out of her mind what had brought her here: abuse and molestation by the ones who raised her, small children born to her at a young age, a husband gone, leaving her to raise the little ones in a dank shack. But her attraction to men, and the raging river of brokenness the molestation had opened, allowed her to stay in the darkness.

Her feet walked the cracked concrete sidewalk, shoes worn thin with a small hole in the seam where cold air filtered in. Two years of prostituting had hardened her. She pulled her coat closer around her frame, the wind whipping her as she struggled to stay upright in the wind. There was nowhere to rest. Trick after trick, she took back to a house owned by a relative. For a cut of the money, he let her use a bedroom to do her business. She shivered and looked up to see the john ahead of her, his dark eyes boring a hole right through her, expectant and waiting. She didn't know how he had found her. She didn't care. She followed him to his home where he roughly grabbed her by the arm and led her through a dark passageway to his back door. She let him, giving into the deep tendrils of darkness that threatened each time she allowed her body to be used.

He escorted her to a dingy bedroom with dense curtains and stale, heavy air. As he stripped her down to nothing, her heart began to race, and her breathing accelerated with fear. The look on his face was menacing and full of rage. He lunged at her, and though startled, she stared at the ceiling, willing it to be over so she could go outside and breathe the damp, cold air. When he was done, she scrambled to her feet to gather her clothes, but with a startling twist of her hair he yanked her hands behind her back and tied them with a rope. She was naked and bound. He led her to another room where he left her carelessly on the floor. He glanced back at her as he went out the door, a smug leer on his face as the heavy bolt clicked into place, leaving her imprisoned inside. Silence emanated from her, and she held her tongue as she knew from experience that to speak would add to any pain. All hope drained away, and she knew why she'd been brought here—to be his sex slave.

She lost track of the days as he raped her repeatedly, and she slipped into a soft space inside her mind—numb to everything around her. Submission, though, came easy to her. To live through the abuse she suffered as a child, it was necessary not to protest. Dim light from the outside world was marked by small slivers of sunlight that shot through the small, cold room. She tried to stay strong, but the act of being strong is harder. Was anyone looking for her? Did anyone care? The horror of each day was filled with hours in a stark room with barely any light, and very little food. Each day she could hear his steps as he made his way to assault her. The smell of him stayed on her, and she couldn't scrub him off, as he kept her dirty and bound.

One afternoon after he was finished with her, the light waning and several weeks having passed, he left her lying helplessly on the floor. He had seemed in a hurry, distracted. Her body ached from the violence. She thought of her kids daily, hourly, and all that was outside this tiny room where she was prisoner. Had this been her fault, being kidnapped and held? Her life, and the choices she had made, were not always the right ones, but she didn't deserve this. A tiny flicker of hope rose in her when he slipped out the door and bolted it. She realized he had forgotten to tie her up.

Not even taking a moment to think, she ran to the window and frantically yanked the curtains off. She paused in fearful anticipation, holding her breath, stillness settling in her bones. The window was grimy and spotted, but she could see light peeking through. Light! Using the heaviest thing she could find, she broke open the window with all the force she could muster and jumped, misgivings left in the room that was her prison, falling heavily to the ground. She jumped up and took off, running down the street, begging for help from anyone who would hear her.

"Help me, please! Someone help me!" Her desperation flooded out through her anguished cries, causing her to lose awareness of her naked and now bloodied body that was covered in bruises and grime—a testament to the torture she had been subjected to.

My name is Jodie. My mom, Judy, was a prostitute and I loved her, even with all she couldn't give me.

This is our story.

Acknowledgments

Billy: I never imagined I would get to live my life with a man who respects and honors me. You are an amazing man for always standing with me and for me. You are so encouraging to me, and I am in awe of you. I am so happy we survived all that was thrown at us. Thank you for not giving up on me. Thank you for being not only an awesome husband but an amazing father and Poppy to our children and grandchildren. I love you more than words can say.

Mindy and Jared: The love I have for you is more than I could ever put into words. You have brought me so much joy. Thank you for loving me in good times and bad. Nothing you could do would ever change the love I have for you. I am so happy with who you both have become. I love you so much, and you both are my favorite.

Thank you to my grandkids, *Chris, Dallas, Paul Jr., Liam, and Rigley*: Oh my, what a love I have for you. I never imagined I could love so much as I love you. Each one of you has brought so much joy to your Nanny and Poppy. We are blessed to call you our grandkids.

To *Val Norton and Priscilla Hamlin*: I love you ladies so much. You have no idea how much you have helped me through your friendship, influence, and counseling through the years. You are my chosen sister and surrogate mother. Thank you for investing in me and my family. I know my mom would have loved you both, and you could have helped her through so much.

My family named and not named, *Kelli*, my dad, *Larry*, and other family members who helped me with details of my mom's life and other details: As a child I could not put things together in my mind. Kelli, Dad, and other family members helped me put those pieces of the puzzle together that I could never have done myself. Thank you to all who helped me with details I did not know. I now see the whole picture.

Break the Grey partners and friends: Thank you for all your support and help. You always encouraged me to write this book and always said JUST DO IT. I thank you for that. I am so blessed with amazing friends from all over the United States and Canada. I love and appreciate you all. *Marissa Purtill,* thank you for encouraging me to press on.

Val Norton, Priscilla Hamlin, Lynn Floyd, Jen Koning, Janice Rigel, Anna Pranger, Renee Andrews, Katrina Clark, Tiffany Burdette, Audra Graber, Tyler Bennett and all my friends who helped me with this book: I appreciate everything you did for me. Taking the time to help me means so much.

Jeff and Dianna Clampitt: I am so thankful for your friendship for all these years. Thankful that Jeff was in that gas station and hired Billy that day in 1989. Thankful that you opened your home to us once we were released from prison. Dianna, I am thankful that you are my best friend and for all the special times we have had over the years. I love you both and your family.

Harlan and Sandy Clampitt: Thank you for being so faithful in visiting me every week I was in prison. For that I so appreciate and love you both.

Joann Ratliff: Thank you for being there for Billy in prison and all your help once we were released. We love you.

Rebekah and Carl Walker and *Mel and Vernell Grantham*: What a true blessing your whole family was right when I needed it. Thank you for the weeklong stay at your beautiful home and for being a blessing to my family. Rebekah, over dinner you and Carl sat me down and blessed me with a brand-new computer and said, "Write your book." I was so blessed that you believed in me and my story.

Barbara Prock and Jim Gillum: We love you both. Thank you for your friendship and hospitality over the years. Barbara, I always enjoyed talking with you. You are a true light of God. Jim, thank you for always supporting Billy in ministry.

To my pastor's, *Bill and Grace Campbell*: Thank you for all your encouragement and teaching through the years. I thank you for showing us love and support and great leadership. We love you.

Jack and Joyce Hayes and Denny and Jackie Keiser: Thank you for allowing Missy and I to use your lake house to write this book. I love and appreciate all that you did for us.

Contents

Acknowledgments

CHAPTER 1

Mom: Little Girl Lost

My mom was born Judith Arminda, with a dreamy middle name that had a movie star quality she could never quite attain. She was born in flat, rough Muncie—the Indiana town she called home— and it remained a place of unflinching pain and struggle for her entire life. She never knew her biological father, as she was always told he had been killed in a car accident when she was one year old. The truth came out later, and she never knew the whole of it. Her father did die, in an auto accident in Kansas, but not until she was nearly five years old. He had divorced her mom when she was two and remarried when she was three. Her mother, my grandmother whom I called Nanny, also remarried that same year as well. There are murky details in between this time that no one knows. It was discovered that my Nanny also had married just after age sixteen to a man thirty years old and was divorced within the year, then marrying my mom's biological dad. By the time Nanny was nineteen she'd been married three times, something we all were kept in the dark about. The last man she married was who I knew as my Papaw.

Nanny was a petite woman, with a cigarette hanging off her lip and a bottle neck beer always in her hand. I remember Papaw in the same way. Nanny worked at Ball State University in the cafeteria, a job she went to every day earning a working woman's wage. Papaw worked for the gas company, and their household was stable as far as finances were concerned.

If you ask different members of the family about them, differing opinions bubble to the surface. One describes Nanny and Papaw's home as a normal household with working parents, nothing out of the ordinary. If you ask another, you'll get an answer like, "I did not like to go over to their house. Your Papaw and other men around were vulgar and said things that should never be said in front of girls and women."

It's easy to hide what goes on inside an insulated frame of a house, stark and still on a patch of land with trees shading its mysterious secrets. From the outside, it can have a normal, cheery coat of paint contradicting the hell-storm that is happening inside. Hell becomes a home for some, and my mother knew that agonizing place from a very young age. Her stepdad, only known to her as her father, slipped into her room at night and little by little took away the very essence of her soul—and her trust of those she loved. With inappropriate sexual touching and hands placed where they should never be on a young child, her normal, everyday life required her to process the abuse he forced on her, causing a chaotic, numbing pain. The resulting sensation became the measure by which all things were deemed true or false to her. She didn't want it, even though she had been subjected to it for more years than she could remember.

She went to her mom with trepidation, praying she would believe her, and tried to tell her what had been happening, but my Nanny wouldn't accept the reality of this abuse from her husband and jumped instantly into a fierce, chosen denial. She looked severely at her daughter Judy through narrowed eyes, and denied it, accusing her of lying. I imagine my mom to have felt deep despair, not to know the loving arms that should comfort, protect, and believe you. What hopelessness and despair my mom must have felt to realize that her own mother would choose not to rescue or deliver her from her nightmare, but rather ignore and deny it to preserve the relationship with her husband. While her stepdad was doing horrific things to her, her childhood bed defiled by his abhorrent behavior, her mom was in a state of disbelief and denial – a suspended, dripping monster of an act that she couldn't – or wouldn't – believe her husband was doing to her child. Bit by bit my mom was shattered and broken by the continuing sexual abuse, as no one believed her. She slipped numbly into a place where she felt no emotion and sadly accepted the hopeless position, she was in. There seemed to be no escape. A fog of paralyzing numbness encapsulated her heart, paving the way to a path of destruction.

It's been said that sexual abuse causes one of two different responses in victims: withdrawing from any type of contact at all, becoming frigid, or becoming dangerously promiscuous. My mother became promiscuous and rebellious—only I would call it a defiance of all that had been inflicted upon her. It was a staunch stand against the forces—my Papaw—that held her, the benefit of the doubt and protection she'd never been given. Are you deemed uncontrollable when childhood abuse traps you with dark vines that bind and twist tightly, choking out everything in its way?

I've often thought that maybe she was lying. My mom died when I was twenty-three at the age of fifty-one, and I can't ask her, can't sit down and chat now that I want to hear the story. I wondered if the abuse story was a way to get attention. A cry for help from a rebellious teen, which is so common to hear. In talking with someone inside the family, poking around for answers to the questions that boiled inside me, there was a startling revelation. "I believe her," said my source, "because he did it to me too." The vindication of that moment was a sweet release, not in the fact that it happened, but that what she had so wanted to share with me was indeed true. My mom had suffered horrific abuse and was never believed.

My mom grew into a teenager, succumbing to and yet surviving the abuse that had befallen her. She was vivacious and full of spirit, with a ready smile. At fourteen, while walking outside after school, she laid eyes on a boy named Kevin who had dark hair and a smile that made her swoon with delight. She was an open book. Most boys and girls at this age notice each other, and my mom was no different. Yet the abuse she suffered had opened her up in an adult way that should never have happened. When she met Kevin, she fell hard and within a few months found herself pregnant with his baby—having my sister Kelli one month after turning sixteen.

In talking with those who knew her then, they describe my mom as a happy person who laughed heartily. When she and Kevin married, she was happy—happier than she had ever been because she was no longer under her dad and his abusive ways. She gave birth to Kelli, and within the year she gave birth to Johnny, two kids in quick succession. But Kevin was not a kind man. He was five years older than Judy and didn't want to be tied down.

Their shack was miniscule, with boards you could see light through, as well as wicked winter winds that swept in with bone-chilling cold. My sister remembers as a tiny child the one room they inhabited, no door to speak of. A heavy, woolen rug was hung over the doorway, passing as a door, and it barely kept the bitter cold out of the room. Pink plastic curtains, waving forlornly in the breeze that sought the inside of the shack, flapped mercilessly. It is a memory firmly etched in her mind. My mom had been happy to be married, though young, but reality soon set in. She was in another prison of her own making. Kevin worked and always had money, but he never spent that money on her or their kids. He left them—abandoned—to fend for themselves.

I want to crawl inside my mom's mind and comfort her when I think about the despair that must have descended on her. She was left behind to survive with two children aged two and one, and herself all of eighteen years old. Kevin's mother stepped in and tried to help, as well as one of his sisters, purchasing shoes from a rummage sale when Johnny started walking. They were desperately poor, and Kevin refused to help them. He's been described as being "tighter than a rubber band" when it came to helping people or sharing—even with his own children. He had no semblance of the normal affection a father should have for his children, and no remorse for leaving them destitute.

I've been told that my mom sank into her own depths of depression and often neglected the children, leaving them in dirty diapers as they cried without comfort. Her dreams for a better life were gone, shattered by a man she didn't realize could have never saved her in the first place. The abuse she suffered by her stepdad, the failed marriage, children she was never equipped to care for...all fell on her like a heavy, wet blanket. Lost in desperation and despair, she gave up her kids to their grandparents—Kelli to her parents and Johnny to her in-laws—because she could no longer care for them.

Lost and alone, she found herself hanging out with shady people who didn't have her best interests at heart, they were masters of persuasion. At all hours she could be found in the lowest places, giving in to the darkness she felt inside her. What was going through her mind? On the streets with no one who cared for her in any real way, she turned to prostitution as easily as she had run into Kevin's arms. It was easy, really. She had grown up saturated in sex from a tiny child. Sex had been normalized.

The Child Welfare League of America says that "Incest is a boot camp for prostitution," and if you looked in my mom's case, you would see that falling into a life of giving herself away was the most accessible path to money. Molestation strips away all confidence and self-worth in a way that can only be understood by the victim. You are a product, a commodity. Sexual exploitation is your life, and it becomes your normal. Prostitution is an easy choice for someone who is already feeling their lowest—abandoned, alone, and overwhelmed in self-contempt. The street became her way of life. Lipstick shining and morale low, she sank into this life of despair resolved that it was the only choice she had. She folded into it as easily as a soft glove fits over your fingers.

My mom tried to make her way back to see her kids several times a month, no matter where she was tricking. She loved them to the degree she was able but lacked the tools to be a nurturing mother in desperate situations. They were unwitting pawns in a game where poverty and hard choices won over common sense. She moved around from town to town, sleeping her way through sketchy places. For a time one of her uncles allowed her to use a bedroom in his home to bring her johns to. Did she enjoy what she was doing? Had it become simply a job that she had dissociated from emotionally? Prostitution let her inner demons out in a way that she could be in control. Being abused and mistreated causes actions that seem out of control to others, but to my mom, it gave her the upper hand. She became voracious and greedy, sucking the life out of men to fill an empty space inside her. Until the day that it didn't.

My mom found herself in Elkhart, Indiana, staying with a relative. Haunting street corners and places where men would find her, she took them to dark and secluded places. She allowed her body to be a vessel, carrying pain and longings. Her own pain was as sharp as the honed edge of a knife, and she let it cut her every day in her quest to live through the assigned minutes of her time; she chose this life.

It was here that she followed the man down the street, her heels click-clacking as her lipstick shone dark under the streetlight. It was here that he assaulted her and took her in ways she had never allowed or known existed—taking away her consent. It was here that he tied her up for weeks in the clandestine spot he had prepared for her. And it was here that she knew it all had to change. When she took her chance after he forgot to tie her, a small mistake he later would regret, and jumped through the smashed window, she ran for her life, her footsteps pounding her way out of an existence that in the beginning she had chosen but knew she must now leave. She made it back to her parents' home, her mom and stepdad's house, where happy times and misery had combined. She was without her kids and had nothing to her name, but she was no longer tied up. She was looking for purpose.

JODIE BALLENGER

MY MOM

MY MOM AND HER FRIEND AFTER HER DIVORCE FROM KEVIN

MY MOM AND HER PARENTS AT HER WEDDING TO KEVIN

CHAPTER 2

Dad: Breaking Bad

Who doesn't want their story to begin well? This one starts somewhere with my paternal grandpa, Charles, going to prison for forgery. The reason behind his actions is lost in the foggy past, as many stories are. Upon release from prison, he went to Ohio to work on his uncle's farm and there met my Grandma Etta, who lived close by. Her family didn't like him, not one bit, because he was a felon. They were a good, solid family who owned a coal business and a small store with a gas station next to their home at the edge of Clifton Gorge State Nature Preserve and the adjoining John Bryan State Park. But love doesn't consider whether a family is good or bad.

My grandpa, Charles Sites, married his love Etta Viola, as found love is never denied no matter the circumstances. Her family disapproved and discouraged her, but she persisted, and they tied the knot in the Midwest of 1930's America. They had four children: Larry (my dad), Betty, Callie, and Lisa. A fifth child, Marcia, came as a surprise much later in their married life. My grandma would soon learn that love wasn't enough to make a happy marriage.

There is sparse information of grandpa's earlier life, and why he was such an authoritarian who ruled the family with an iron fist. They lived in Muncie, Indiana, and my dad and his sister, Betty, would stand on street corners and sell newspapers for five cents a paper, saving their money in dime banks. Soon after World War II ended, my grandpa heard of work in Galveston, Texas. He managed to buy a '36 Oldsmobile, and all six of them packed into it like sardines and headed to the coast. My dad doesn't remember what work his father, Charles, did there, only that they lived in that car; living every day out in that car. He recalls the sand on the beach in Galveston, his dad having driven the car too close to the waves of the ocean. He was cleaning it, washing the grit off, and the waves took that sand right out from under the tires, and they were stuck. My grandpa had to pay to get the car towed out of the sand.

The memories are foggy, but they left Galveston and drove up the coast, rounding Texas into Louisiana, Mississippi, and Alabama, and on into Florida through Georgia, ending up in

West Columbia, South Carolina. There they lived in a trailer and stayed long enough to start school, which his sisters faithfully attended, but dad remembers not going. "I was a little rascal," he said. His father whipped him when he found out he wasn't attending school, but it didn't matter, for they soon left and beat a trail to Oklahoma.

It was the beginning of many trails taken. A ranch awaited them there, where Dad and Grandpa Charles worked in the fields shucking corn. My grandma and aunts worked in apple orchards, plentiful and green, the round juicy orbs falling into bushel baskets while their arms ached from reaching. The owners of the ranch had a company store. As the song goes, "I owe my soul to the company store," and dad's family soon owed them that much and more. The store had groceries, necessities, and everything you could need, which you bought on credit, taking it off your earnings as you worked. They earned $18 per week—not enough for a family of six—putting them in the negative from day one and owing more than they ever made. To pay off the debt, they left the Oldsmobile and started walking—all the way to Kansas.

I imagine my dad and his family walking those dusty roads. He remembers sleeping in jails at night, the welcome relief of a solid floor to lay weary heads on. When they arrived at their destination, a vast acreage of cotton fields somewhere in Kansas, they stayed for two or three years, working different farms. Cotton picking is back-breaking work, and my dad makes the distinction between "picking" and "pulling" cotton. When you pull cotton, the whole pod is pulled off, whereas picking is retrieving the cotton from the pods, which paid much less. Toil and exhaustion—that's what my dad mostly remembers from his early years.

It wasn't all bad, those days at home with his dad, mom, and sisters; there were some good moments he tries to put a finger on. Grandpa Charles, though, could be mean and demanding. Dad became nearly deaf in one ear from being slapped in the head repeatedly over the years. Grandma Etta couldn't defend my dad, or any of her kids, as she too would become the target. Emotionally and physically, they were under grandpa's thumb. I try to see it through her eyes, her love for him, yet the spiraling realization that her choice had wrought such dire circumstances—no comfort to be found in the love she once felt.

Learning a Trade

Sioux Falls, South Dakota, became the next destination on Grandpa Charles' radar. There they lived in a tent, summer and winter, and South Dakota where winters are known to be bone-chilling cold. They lived near a huge park that had herds of buffalo, a place where all five kids loved to marvel at nature. For my dad, this is where he was taught to be a thief. Had my grandpa been a thief before all this? Probably so, and he taught them how to sneak up on the other side of cars when people would get out to play with their children. Dad and Aunt Betty would slip in and steal the money right out of their purses and give it to grandpa. Grandma noticed but never said anything to anger her husband. That would be worse than chastising her kids for stealing.

They did this often, becoming skilled at what they did, but not so good that the police didn't finally catch them red-handed and load them up in the police car. Grandma and grandpa came looking for them at the park they'd dropped them off at earlier in the day to do their dirty deeds of stealing from the cars of unsuspecting tourists. That's when my grandparents saw their kids waving to them from the back of a police car. They didn't follow them, their own kids, to the station. They slunk back to the tent where the cops eventually brought their kids back to. To this day my dad doesn't know whether the cops even mentioned to his parents what they had been caught doing. It didn't matter because soon after they left South Dakota, hitchhiking and walking, zig-zagging around for a bit at friends' and relatives' places, then coming back to Muncie, Indiana, for good. When they arrived in Indiana, my dad was fourteen years old. The year was 1949.

To be a thief you must be stealthy and swift, and the lifestyle had gotten under my dad's skin. Packs of cigarettes were ten cents back in the early '50s and cartons ran a dollar. Dad would slink inside cars and steal cigarettes as well as anything else that looked like it needed to be taken. He had become an expert at what he did, but people started noticing that things were missing from their cars, and the police were alerted to look out for young juveniles with sticky fingers. One day they caught my dad with a stolen carton of cigarettes and took him home to turn in to his parents.

When they got to the small house, the police decided to search it. What they found caused the biggest rift in Dad's family. Grandpa Charles had been storing rifles, guns, and other stolen property underneath a bed. It was a secret no one had known about. "They found everything underneath the one bed," says my dad, "and they got us all."

And just like that my grandpa and grandma were sent to prison for six months, for receiving stolen goods, and the family was torn apart. I imagine my grandma's horror, regretting the decisions that had brought her to this place, mourning for her children. The girls went to Muncie Children's Home, and when my grandma and grandpa got out six months later, they were able to get the girls back. But my dad was older, fifteen at the time, and was sentenced to three years in the Indiana

Boys School, an institution to which youthful offenders are sent as an alternative to prison. The mission of a reform school is to do just that: reform you. There were trades you could learn so you could be a productive citizen when you were let out. Dad started out in plumbing then moved on to doing what was called "workouts," which meant working outside the school at different places of business. He worked on a tree farm, then at a coal company, earning at most three dollars a day. He recalls enjoying that money made and ordering a cake and a case of pop every weekend as a reward, as well as to share it with the other boys there who were not as fortunate as he. He quit school in the tenth grade to focus on working every day, but he played on the basketball team while there. "I didn't get into high school" he says, laughing.

Reformed or not, my dad got out, and it wasn't long before he found himself in trouble with the law. It flows thick and deep, that rush you get when you know what you're doing isn't the right thing. It's a thrill, a high, and something that's hard to get past when you don't have much going for you in your life. He was caught during a burglary and found himself in the Indiana State Farm. He did his time and, with two weeks to go in his sentence, found out they were transferring him to Morgan Monroe State Park as a trustee, where he knew they would make him cut down trees. He didn't want to cut down trees, so he told them, in all sincerity, "If you make me go, I'll leave." They transferred him, and that night he escaped, crossing the Ohio River into Cincinnati to stay with his sister Lisa and her husband.

Dad was an escapee, on the run, and he stayed in the Cincinnati area for a while before going up to Fort Wayne, Indiana, to see his parents. While there he borrowed his father's car and wrecked it, handed back the keys, which were all that was left of the car, took off and hitchhiked from Fort Wayne to West Virginia. He had no money and had not eaten for days. He was so desperately hungry that he turned himself in and was taken to Pendleton Reformatory, where he was given a one- to five-year sentence. He served three years and would have gotten off on less had he had good behavior. "Every time I was ready to go on parole, I'd be leading the parade going to the hole," he says. "It took me three years to get out, but I could've gotten out in one. I was ornery. I was mean."

If marriage and children were the answer to walking the straight and narrow, then my dad missed the message. He married a woman named Marcia and within a few years two children were born to them, Larry Jr and Becky. However, the life he had lived came calling—had never really left. He craved a life filled with tightrope tension. Leaving his wife and kids at home many times over, he sought excitement drinking at bars. Rough nights and the thrill of doing whatever he wanted became a dark shadow that chased him relentlessly through life.

Consequences

My dad found himself in a small town across the Ohio state line late one night, carousing and up to no good. He entered and sat down in a bar, drinking beer and thinking of ways he could make some money, ways that weren't by working for an honest wage. He left the bar late, biding his time until it shut down for the night. It was dark, a night where the stars hide and any sliver of moon that peeks out is quickly vanquished by clouds. The cigarette he puffed on sent small rings up through the night sky, the tree he sat behind shielding it from view. He could hear his breath catch in his throat, tamping down the misgivings he had when a plan came to fruition. He waited, and when all was silent and still at the bar, he crossed the parking lot, slinking like a cat. He looked through a small window and saw that all was clear.

Jimmying the lock was easier than he'd imagined, and he slipped inside the bar. The floors were littered with refuse from the previous hours, awaiting a broom the next day. He looked down the rows of stools and saw glasses stacked inside a rubber container, waiting to be cleaned for thirsty mouths. The pool table loomed in the darkness as he popped the lock on the coin slot to retrieve the quarters. He popped the lock on the cigarette machine as well, filling his pockets full of quarters with a smirk on his face. A thief is just that, a thief, who has but a singular purpose and means to an end. Yet to be a good thief you must be wary and cover all bases, and here is where my dad failed. At the end of the bar was a large square window he had not noticed in his hurry to find money. As he was taking money from the cash register, he lifted his head and a chill ran down his spine as he glanced to his left.

He couldn't clearly identify the sensation that hit him. An explosion of glass, along with the deafening sound of a gunshot, rang out, piercing his eardrums. It was lightning quick, and he was overwhelmed with excruciating pain as the bullet entered the edge of his temple and plunged into his eye, lodging in the bone in his nose. Two more gunshots followed; this time he was struck in the front of his nose and his neck. He grabbed his eye and doubled over in shock and agony, realizing the owner of the bar had been watching him through the square window and took his chance when he was unaware.

Unable to logically comprehend his crisis adequately in his state of shock, my dad bolted out the closest door, racing to his vehicle parked down the road. Blood was gushing from his face as he jumped behind the wheel and fumbled for his keys, the bar owner in hot pursuit. He spun his tires and sped away with the owner having reached his own car as well. He was tailing him hot and heavy, gravel and dust billowing in clouds behind them. Somewhere on the flat stretches of Northwest Ohio, Dad outran the owner of that bar, leaving him in frustration, his gun still smoking beside him.

As if things couldn't get any worse, Dad's car stalled along the highway. He abandoned it in a panicked shock and walked, staggering nearly three miles with his eye hanging out of his eye socket when he finally spotted a truck stop. His adrenaline had numbed his pain and desperation had motivated him to fight for his life. His face a mangled mess, swollen and full of coagulating blood. He looked like a monster with one eye, a creature of the night. When he staggered into the truck stop a shocked hush came over the place, and they stared in horror. Once they recovered from the sight, realizing he needed help, the waitresses frantically rushed about to give him towels for his face. Questions were fired at him in a frenzy: What happened? Should we call the police? Who did this to you? Should we call an ambulance? Dad scrambled for answers in his shocked stupor and fabricated a story that he had been beaten up, but that no, he didn't need the police. Lying, he said that he knew who had done this to him and they wouldn't want the police involved. His head pounding and full of lead, it wasn't long before a truck driver offered to take him to his sister's home across the Indiana line.

The miles stretched on, and when he finally arrived at Aunt Lisa's house, she looked at him in panic and demanded that he go to the hospital. He finally gave in, realizing that his injuries were too great to bear without medical attention. He was in the hospital for three days. He lost his eye that night.

The details of the bar incident had been discovered by police, the owner telling all, and Dad was scheduled to go to court in Ohio. Thank God, the bullets were just a little bigger than BBs. He had healed nicely from the shooting and was awaiting the court date in Ohio when the itch began again—the itch to scratch a surface better left untouched. The night before the court date in Ohio, my dad attempted another burglary and was caught immediately. They transported him to Ohio, where the judge told him they had arranged for probation for the bar break-in, but considering the new burglary attempt they had changed their minds. He was given one to twenty years at the Ohio State Prison in Columbus. He was released after two years, but not before Marcia divorced him. She had had enough.

He floated around aimlessly for a couple of weeks until he went to Muncie to visit family. And that's where he met my mom.

JODIE BALLENGER

PRISON PHOTO OF MY DAD (LARRY)

CHAPTER 3

Hurting People
Hurt People

As fate would have it, Mom was in the same town at the same time. Several weeks had passed since she escaped her captor, and she was still reeling from her horrifying experience, trying to regain some semblance of a normal life. But never having had what you call a "normal" life left her raw and open to negative influence and someone offering some semblance of stability. My dad says, "They told me not to mess with her. Said she was bad news, but I messed with her."

What was mom thinking when she met my dad? I long to ask her, to sit and chat over coffee about what her feelings had been. Was she looking for someone to care for her and protect her? I believe so. My mom was attracted to men who leaned on the hard side of life. The danger was enticing and mesmerizing to her, and my dad was right up her alley. Not long after that they were married. Nothing could stop them. All the warnings and words meant to keep them apart because of who the other might be didn't stop them. Dad was a divorced father of two, and mom was a divorced mother of two. Prison, prostitution, and abandonment to lives filled with dangerous, fast living had led them to find each other in their mutual dysfunction.

Marriage began for them on a wing and a prayer in 1964, and they settled in Fort Wayne, Indiana. My mom wanted her children Kelli and Johnny back, but the grandparents they had been staying with didn't want to let them go. They hesitated with concern, acknowledging that the life she had been living was dangerous for the kids. But when she married my dad, even with his criminal record and three stints in the pen, they let them return. I believe my mom thought if she had a new man, who would help with the children, she could manage to parent again. I also believe that because of the lack of love and affection in her own childhood, somehow she thought her children could fill that love deficit and finally help her feel loved. But being raised in the cycle of abuse, and trying to navigate her way out of it, didn't leave my mom with the skill set, for example, on how to raise children. She settled in, freshly married, to attempt to make it work.

Dad and Mom, if anything, were a good time. Mom smoked two packs of cigarettes a day, and my dad was a weekend drunk. The tavern was their favorite place to hang out, and every Friday and Saturday night that's where you could find them. My dad became a good provider and always had enough money to pay the bills and keep food on the table, as well as for Mom's gambling addiction, her downfall.

Believe it or not, Mom wanted more children and tried for years to have them. Finally, she became pregnant with my older sister, Adrian—born in December 1968—and the very next year, December 1969, I made my entrance into a world I wasn't quite ready for.

My parents' relationship was a volatile one. My dad cheated on my mom frequently throughout their relationship. My sister Kelli remembers various occasions that they found our dad with other women. My mom cheated on him as well. Her vicious nature and simmering rage came out in ferocious ways. Was this an expected behavior to her? Did she believe this was a normal way of relating in marriage? I'm uncertain as to whether she thought it was part of the marriage experience or not. They persisted, both testing and trying the waters of marriage, stumbling through infidelities and demeaning behavior.

My mom was humorous at times, a poker player, vulgar and very open about sex and all that went along with it. She made you want to be around her, for her to gather you into her dysfunction like a broken toy. She drew people magnetically to her who were not in a healthy emotional state themselves, people who were seeking someone to feed their own insecurities and codependency. I grew up loving my mom in the most desperate way, even though I knew she wasn't taking care of me like most moms do. She didn't know how to love in a nurturing way; I knew she wanted to, but she simply didn't know how. She had a way of staying distant emotionally and relationally, yet physically near. It was puzzling for someone so young as I was. When I was three years old, my mom divorced my dad. They got remarried two years later. They were erratic and irresponsible yet full of passion and rage. They were an unsolved mystery to me.

Some stray memories of good things and happy moments have stayed with me. I remember waking up very early one Christmas morning, when I was three or four years old, and opening gifts at home around a tree. We had gotten up early so we could go to my mom's parents, Nanny and Papaw's house, later that morning. One of my favorite pictures of my dad—hanging in my living room—is of this Christmas morning. I can remember the anticipation and excitement I felt as that little girl, looking forward to Christmas and what it would bring. I have pictures of me unwrapping my present at Nanny and Papaw's that morning. As I eagerly unwrapped that gift, I was overwhelmed with a sense of wonder and awe when a doll emerged from the wrapping as tall as me! I was so excited about this doll I could barely contain it. In that moment, I felt a brief awareness of being loved. I soaked it up like a thirsty sponge.

Another Christmas I remember happened a few years later when I was five or six. We woke up to a living room filled with toys and little cars that we could ride in, the ones you had to peddle to make them go. I was so filled with wonder and excitement. Later that day we were headed as a family over to friends of my parents to play poker, and we were told to pick one of our presents that we could take along to play with. I picked a baby doll. On our way home that evening a violent fight brewed in the car, deep and heavy between my parents. My mom was furious.

"I demand you let me out of this car now! Stop this car!" she shouted vehemently. Angrily, Dad stopped the car so abruptly it caused us kids to be thrust forward harshly, and Mom grabbed me roughly by the arm and made me go with her. There we were, Christmas Day, in the middle of nowhere watching Dad race away in the car. I watched forlornly as he drove away, confused and bewildered and aching from the emotional whiplash of the day's unexpected events. We started walking down the road. I was baffled as to why the day had started off so incredible and ended so dreadful. But there was no explanation given. Someone in the family picked us up as we were walking and took us home.

I knew that day that to stay on her good side was the wisest choice. However, this was a challenge I rarely succeeded at. The rules were constantly changing.

Two Realities

These almost dream-like remembrances are set side by side with memories of my mom's violent outbursts. It was like there were two realities for us: Reality A and Reality B. Reality B was a scary, violent, and horrendous place to be. It never made logical sense, and there was no pleasing her in reality B, no matter how desperately we tried. Reality A was when she was kind and actually seemed to care for us. I learned from a young age that she couldn't control her temper and would batter whatever child had upset her in Reality B. She used switches, wire coat hangers, or anything she could grab. Her eyes would change in those moments, as if a button had been pressed, transforming her into a monstrous force. A hard and hungry edge came over her face that terrified me enough that I learned to block it out. Her words were as wounding as her physical abuse in those Reality B times. I didn't want to remember Reality B, with the ugly sides of her. Because of this, I repressed many of these memories somewhere in the deepest recesses of my mind. She reveled in the violence, letting it rumble through her body with a raging vengeance.

My eldest sister, Kelli, remembers the beatings as well when Mom would grow weary of us younger two girls. "When she got tired of you two girls, I had to take care of you," she says, stating facts plainly. "Many times, she made me stay home from school because she had stayed up all night and wanted to sleep." The school would contact our mom day after day inquiring about why Kelli was absent, and finally Mom would allow Kelli to go back to school.

When my elder siblings, Kelli and Johnny, were young, and my mom tired of taking care of them, she would send them to their biological father's house. "We were constantly back and forth," Kelli explains, "and we quickly learned we were not welcome at our dad and stepmom's house. This made our overnight visits awkward and extremely stressful. Our mom was not a mom. She wasn't meant to be one."

It is sad to me when a father is nothing more than a sperm donor to a child, and the birth mother or stepmother is nothing more than a physical presence with little semblance of nurture, protection, or affection. Children are so often thrust into situations with stepparents that want nothing to do with them, and no one cares enough to notice or help. They knew clearly that when they went to their dad Kevin's home with his wife, they weren't welcome. Kelli felt that she and Johnny would have been better off if Mom had left them with their grandparents where they were both loved and well taken care of. If only my mom would have known that her selfishness in wanting her children back, even though it was not in their best interest, would be the beginning of a road that would lead one of them down a painful, destructive path that would ultimately claim their life... Kelli said she was never abused in any way from my Papaw.

The lack of care had serious effects that started when I was very young. The succession of the next stories I'll relate are the beginning of what was to be my life. A foundation of incest and abuse is a crumbling one, and my mom carried her baggage around with her from each place to the next. Incest and molestation are truly a boot camp for prostitution, addiction, sexual abuse, and neglect in the home. For my family, it would be a textbook we would learn from for years to come.

Innocence Stolen

Memories come to my mind, and to describe them in detail is not hard. I was four, and the house we lived in had a firepit in the backyard. It was a wooded area where trees seemed taller than the sky to a small child. Johnny and Kelli had some friends over to the house, and like all small siblings, I wanted to be around where the action was. They would have been just into high school, the age where everything and everyone is annoying to you. Even though I was innocent and naive, soon my innocence would be stolen and defiled in a way no child's ever should be. One of my brother and sister's friends molested me in snatches of private moments—touched me repeatedly where I shouldn't have been touched. During these times of touching and others just like it, I was groomed by the molester. Most of the time it was the "tickling game" that started out fun and ended with his hands in private places. He lured me with the promise that it would be fun, and I would enjoy it, and it did start out fun, but it shifted quickly into something that was not fun at all. I remember his hands invading and feeling very uncomfortable. I was so young and didn't understand what was happening, but the memory was etched deep in my soul in a way that began to build an identity of being used, abused, and embracing the lie that this was the foundational definition of what I was worth.

My oldest sister Kelli, who was like my second mom, was now married and moving to Muncie with her husband. She was very young, only in tenth grade at the time. When her husband came to get her to move and they were putting things in the back of his truck, I hid inside the back of the truck to go along with her. My bond with Kelli is something I can't adequately explain. She helped raise me, and I felt as if I were losing her now that she was going away. I remember feeling abandoned and desperately wanting her to stay or take me with her. Sadly, it didn't take long for Kelli to find out that her husband was cheating on her, continuing the family cycle established in multiple generations. Their marriage ended in short order, and she moved back to Fort Wayne and rented a room in the house right next to the one we had just moved to. If it's wrong to say I was happy she was back, then let it be wrong. My little girl's heart rejoiced that she had returned!

At our new home, older neighbor girls lived across the street, and I looked up to them—you know how you're in awe of "older girls" when you're young? Their age ranged from a few years older than me to early teen. They were fascinating to me, so I was so excited when they asked me to come over to their house and included me in their circle. In their bedroom, they started doing sexual things to each other, making it look fun and inviting.

"You want to do this too, don't you, Jodie?" they asked, enticing me strategically. At four, you go along with what the big kids are doing. They began to touch me sexually, laughing and goading me into enjoying it. I remember thinking, even at that young age, *Why does this keep happening to me?* I didn't understand what was wrong with me that made people do these things to me. I had only wanted to be a small part of their cool older-girl-world, but instead I was taught something that would never leave me and continue to form the defective definition of my self-worth.

Several of my older boy cousins, on different occasions, molested me as well, perpetuating what I began to think about myself, a certain vein of "truth" that threaded through my life. Did I have a sign on my forehead that said "Touch me"? I didn't understand, and after a while this type of fondling stopped surprising or even shocking me.

I have a memory of when my mom and I visited one of her friend's home, where they sat at the table smoking and chattering all afternoon. My mom's friend had a son who was six, a year or so older than me. We were playing around the house as children do and entered his bedroom. Soon after, a kissing session began, and his mom abruptly walked in on us. She immediately grew enraged, yelling at me. What had I done wrong? Wasn't this normal? Wasn't this what you were supposed to do? Why was she so angry? Suddenly, what I had begun to believe was normal was maliciously defined as morally shameful and abhorrent, and what's more, it was all my fault. I was to blame. It wasn't her anger that stayed with me, though. What I took away from this moment was that my mom didn't defend me or protect me. She was wooden, aloof, disconnected, as if expecting this to happen, and my feeling of being alone in that moment adheres to me like a sticky spider's web to this day.

My mom had always wanted more babies, even though she was unable to take care of the ones she had. She suffered many health issues, from diabetes to heart problems, and was in and out of the hospital at least a couple of times a year—as far back as I can remember. A neighbor who lived across the street from us learned that she was pregnant, and she planned to give the child away for adoption. My mom decided she wanted that baby—wanted it badly—and she pleaded with the neighbor to let her have it, raise it, care for it. My dad was concerned that in a year or so the birth mom would come back and try to take the baby away from them, so he came up with a solution. He talked to the neighbor, and it was decided that my dad's name would go on the birth certificate as the father. That way he would be the legal father, and no one could say otherwise. Both my mom and dad were there when the baby, a little girl, was born, and were with her when Dad's name was decreed on the birth certificate. Then he put that baby in his car, after she was released from the hospital, and drove with my mom and new baby sister home to us. Just like that. The neighbor moved somewhere, my dad recalls, maybe California. And this is how my little sister Lucy came to be with us.

Unfortunately, having children doesn't fix what's already wrong in the home, or with the people living inside it who are living, breathing individuals with deep soul wounds and bruises from their lives. Our home had a heavy dose of bruising. I've said before that my dad was a relentless ladies' man and that this side of him was an ugly part of who he was. I was in the third grade, that fall of 1979, when my world really turned upside down. We came home from school, fall winds still breezy in early November, and walked into a house that had been normal when we left. Now nearly everything we owned was packed into a U-Haul truck that sat filled to the brim in our driveway.

My heart stopped in fear as I looked around for my parents, an explanation, or anything to calm me. Mom came from another room, looked at us, and said nonchalantly, "We're moving." She was urgent in her tone yet determined in her movements. Her no-nonsense side had kicked in. My dad took our hands and walked us outside and drove us to a convenience store at the end of the block in eerie silence. Our confusion and panic were apparent, and he wanted to try to explain as best he could.

"Girls, I don't want you to go. I love you," he said. "But this is something I can't stop. Maybe one day you'll understand."

I looked at his face and saw the hint of tears, his glass eye immobile, and the other eye watery and full of emotion. What I didn't know then, couldn't know, was that my mom had caught him with someone close to us, someone off limits, someone who shocked even her. In that moment, there had been clarity, a veil of denial pulled back, and she had packed up our things in one day. Abandonment and betrayal deepened once again and developed a stranglehold on my wounded soul that day. We left our dad that night—Mom, my sisters, and myself—and moved on to another world where I would continue down a dangerous and rocky road that had been set before me, without my consent.

MOM AND DAD ON THEIR WEDDING DAY WITH MY GREAT GRANDMA
GOLDIE

DAD MOM KELLI & JOHNNY

DAD AND MOM EARLY IN THEIR MARRIAGE

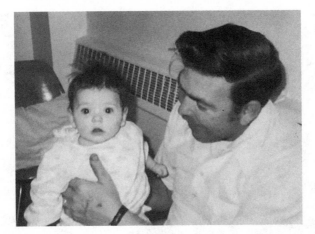

DAD AND ME

MOM AND ME

JODIE BALLENGER

ME AT CHRISTMAS

MOM DAD & ME

ADRIAN DAD ME

MY FAVORITE CHRISTMAS MEMORY WITH MY DAD

JODIE BALLENGER

FAIR TIME—Four-year-old Jody Sites, who lives in the Nebraska neighborhood, and her Pomeranian, Reefer, were among the crowd Saturday.—Staff photo by John Sorensen.

ADRIAN KELLI JOHNNY ME DAD MOM LUCY

• 44 •

CHAPTER 4

Living in a Drug House

Cleveland, Ohio—that was our destination. It seemed exciting, driving away with all our things jammed in the back. I tried to view it as a kind of adventure seen through my nine-year-old eyes. Profoundly sad that we were leaving my dad, but excited to be moving in with my cousins, I wanted to ask my mom why we were leaving, and maybe I did, but I don't remember ever getting a clear answer from her.

My sister Kelli had now married her second husband, and they had my niece Karen who had just turned three years old. We had just celebrated her birthday before we left. My brother Johnny was now nineteen and out of the house. I believed that to be a real family you must stay together no matter what, and I wished with all my heart it was so. The lives of the adults in my sphere of existence perplexed me, so I stopped asking the whys. None of their answers made sense, if they ever answered me at all.

We stayed overnight at a hotel—a rare treat—on the way to Cleveland, sleeping in the next morning and feeling rich for a few hours. Pulling into Cleveland that afternoon, the city stretched out before us, and I could see how enormous it was.

"Doesn't it look pretty?" Mom said. We gazed in wonder. It did indeed look beautiful, new and exciting. The beauty of the city quickly evaporated into a vision of poverty and want. We pulled up in front of the house and tumbled out of the vehicle and into my aunt's home, my mom's youngest sister. The house had an upstairs apartment, and someone was living there when we arrived. We lived with my aunt and her family on the first floor for a few weeks.

I was overcome with excitement because there were cousins everywhere. It didn't take very long to realize that it may not be as thrilling as I expected. I opened the refrigerator expecting to see food, and what I saw took my breath away: mason jars stacked to the brim with pills. Little ones, big ones, pink ones, and yellow ones. All kinds of pills were in that refrigerator. The colors mesmerized me as I took them in. I wasn't sure why my uncle had them, but I didn't want to ask him. My uncle was mean, meaner than a hungry alley cat. Every single day he got up and went to his job as a garbage man, riding the trucks that picked up the trash on the east side of Cleveland. At the end of the shift he would bring home boxes of donuts and other things he had salvaged out of the trash, food he felt was still good to eat. My cousins never missed a beat and scooped that food up like it was gold, but I hesitated, grossed out and unsure if I could ever eat this way.

When the other people moved out upstairs, we moved in. It was a tiny apartment with a miniscule kitchen and living room, and a door off the kitchen led to an attached attic portion. The floors were unfinished in this attic room we slept in, and they laid down plywood so we could lay our mattresses down to sleep. The catch was we had to be careful not to step where there was no plywood, or we would fall straight through the beams and into my aunt's house. Precarious, to say the least.

The first night we stayed in Cleveland, Mom treated us to sub sandwiches. The kids played in the living room as the adults smoked something my mom called wacky tobacky, funny rolled cigarettes that smelled weird, as they caught up with each other in the kitchen. Later that evening, I fell asleep in the makeshift beds they had made for us on the floor, having eaten half of the sandwich. I woke up in the middle of the night, still hungry and disoriented. I picked up the sandwich and put it to my mouth, munching away. In the morning, I woke up shocked and repulsed to see the sandwich covered in roaches. All I could think about was that I had picked up that sandwich in the middle of the night and was eating it. My stomach turned sickeningly with the thought. I had never seen roaches before, and it disgusted me to think they were on the sandwich. I shuddered and made a mental note to NEVER eat food that had been left out again!

My uncle was intimidating and frightening, and he towered over us. He didn't like my mom, and my mom didn't like him. I can remember him charging upstairs in a rage to yell at my mom or sister, his face angry and red. They could never hold back their words and were always on the wrong side of his anger. I, on the other hand, was so terrified of him that I tried to stay out of his way, tried to make myself invisible. He reminded me of Brutus on *Popeye*.

My uncle's mom and many of his relatives lived next door in Grandma June's house. They turned her house into two homes and separated the families for a bit more privacy. A driveway was the only thing that separated the two homes, barely a hair's breadth apart. My uncle's sister lived in the house behind us with her three kids. I loved to play with my cousins at Grandma June's when I stayed there, and I stayed there a lot. Grandma June was kind to me and treated me like I was her granddaughter. June worked at the Amvets thrift store across the street where she was the manager. The wonderful part of that was that we could go there, like a pack of wild dogs, and pick out anything we wanted. I was able to get new-to-me clothes this way. It felt like Christmas!

Some of my cousins and I visited a church down the street several times, and I loved how they were so kind to us. There was something different about the people at this church that fascinated me. I would recall this years later, in even more desperate times.

The teacher's strike of 1979 occurred when we moved to Cleveland. The strike was so big they shut down most of the Cleveland public schools, including the one a few blocks away that we should have been attending. That meant time to run around, investigate, and check out our new territory. I tried to keep out of my uncle's way, but the area was small, and we kids—eleven of us between all three houses—were running in and out like chickens with our heads cut off. I discovered that the pills in the fridge were just the tip of the iceberg. Three huge black trash bags filled with marijuana sat in my uncle and aunt's bedroom. In addition, the blocks of hashish they had were big, and they would cut them up fine and sell it to people. They were drug dealers, and not small-time drug dealers at that. They were in deep. Within a week of our arrival, I was smoking pot daily. My cousins and I would take handfuls and stick it in baggies, stuffing it in our pockets the way we saw the adults do. We also snuck pills out of the refrigerated mason jars, whichever ones looked pretty, and popped them for the rush. I was taking pills and getting high every day. I was nine years old.

Recently a drug enforcement agent estimated the worth of those three huge trash bags of marijuana at $200,000, and that didn't include the brick of hashish and mason jars full of pills. The east side of Cleveland was a dangerous neighborhood and very scary to me. Near the house we lived in, they found a woman's body one day in a field littered with trash. But we were kids, so we pushed down the fear and chose to forget, running with abandon in those dirty, gritty streets.

One of those times we ran through the backyard, into my aunt's neighbor's patchy yard, and up into a tree that looked perfect for climbing. Up, up we went until we were perched on the branches where we could look out over the neighborhood. *Bang! Bang!* Shots rang out, and we turned in horror to see our aunt's neighbor angrily shooting at us and calling us racial names. We scrambled down as fast as we could as he raged, gun in hand. I never ran so fast in my life! My aunt came running out and yelled at him to stop. We never climbed his tree again.

Mom knew the neighborhood was shady and dangerous, and I remember her muttering day after day, "I need a gun. I need to buy a gun." One day there was a knock at the door, and she rushed to it quickly. I saw a man standing there, shifting his weight from one foot to the other, as if he were anxious, in a hurry. She invited him into the kitchen, and I saw him take out a gun and my mom press money into his hand. He handed her the gun and she slipped it in her purse, closing the door. She looked at me expressionless, knowing I had observed everything.

The trail of sexuality pursued close behind me and didn't end when I arrived in Cleveland. I was soon involved with a cousin. Our hands were wildly active upon both our bodies, as I had already normalized this type of behavior. The term "kissing cousins" opened an entirely new landscape that I couldn't and didn't want to escape from. My mom and her open sexual ways had rubbed off on me.

My uncle continued to be furious all the time and seemed to have a short fuse that burned white-hot. When school started up again after the strike ended, I was glad to get away from him and his unbridled anger. I trudged along to school with my cousins and started classes at the elementary school. I soon noticed that my cousins, a few others, and I were the only white kids at this school. The other students made sure we were aware of this fact too. At this school, it wasn't cool to be white. I felt the intense discomfort, as well as the loneliness, but wanted to make it work by being brave.

The district we were in was one of the poorest in the city. One day the principal called us into an assembly where hundreds of shoes, the same style, were handed out to every single child in the school. This was a foreign concept to me because back in Fort Wayne we always had nice clothes and shoes and plenty of food. Here in Cleveland, we hadn't yet descended into the abject poverty that we would, and so I still separated myself in my mind. "We're not poor!" I told myself indignantly. "So why would I need these shoes?" I was mortified and took them home and placed them stubbornly on a shelf. I never wore them. Even being on food stamps, once we got to Cleveland, I still didn't consider our family poor. We would take our stamps down the block to a store where you could buy anything—not just food—with your book of food stamps. It was an illegal operation, to be sure, but it worked out quite nicely for the neighborhood.

After a week or so at the school I had grown to hate it. I decided to speak to my mom about it. "Mom, could I switch to another school?" I begged. "I hate this school! It's awful! The kids pick on us, and it's so scary. Please, Mom, can we change schools?" My heart raced as I hoped she would listen for once and move me from that school. Surprisingly, she agreed with me and quickly enrolled me in a different school, several blocks away from the hated one. I wanted to believe wholeheartedly for it to be better and to like it, but it was no different. The disappointment I felt snatched away my last ray of hope to attend a school I liked and felt safe at.

After the first day at this new school, I was waiting on the steps to be picked up. Mom wasn't there yet, she was running late, and two little girls rushed up to me with a threatening air. "We don't want you here. You don't belong here," they said, muttering angrily more insulting racial terms and literally spitting in my face. The emotional devastation I felt was like being kicked in the gut, and the next building block was added to the ever-growing foundational definition of my worth that told me I was unwanted and opened my eyes to racism. When my mom finally arrived, too late to rescue me from what I had experienced, I jumped into the car and burst into tears. I never went back. I was exposed young to up-close and in-your-face prejudice. I eventually learned that there are good people and bad people in all races and religions. It is not a one-sided issue, it is all sides. I experienced it firsthand. Let's end prejudice and racism by ending it with ourselves first.

A Place I Loved

As it happened, after being shuffled from place to place and giving up hope that I would ever find a place and people to fit in with, my mom met a man named Austin who was a Tohono O'odham native American, formally known as the Papago Indians. The Papago tribe is in the Arizona desert, extending down into the Sonoran Desert of Mexico. Austin became a safe place to me, someone who "saw" me, really took the time to know me and love me for who I was—Jodie. Even though he was an alcoholic and in an adulterous relationship with my mom, still he was so kind. He was what you would describe as a "nice drunk," someone who laughed and smiled and didn't verbally or physically abuse people. My mom fell hard for him, and soon we all moved out and found an upstairs apartment in a Latino neighborhood with Austin.

I couldn't get enough of the feelings this change brought me. For the first time I could crawl out of the protective numb cocoon I had created around myself to shut down emotions of pain I experienced at every turn and couldn't escape from. The atmosphere was friendlier here, the area was nicer, and the people were kind and loving. Was this for real? Could I really trust it? Or would it all collapse as a sick joke just when I began to hope that perhaps I had discovered authentic people who cared and were safe? Did I dare to let the walls down? I loved that in this neighborhood my mom took the time with me and my baby sister to go for walks. People were so friendly and sociable, sitting outside with their Latino music playing, and waved to us as we walked by. This was so refreshing to me as a child who had just left a roach-infested drug house.

There was a little storefront Mexican restaurant that we went to sometimes, and I thought as a child that I could live there forever. The school I was enrolled at here is a place I will never forget. I only wish I had been able to go there longer. Inside the big yellow brick building were interior glass walls facing a courtyard. I was in awe of those walls and the crystal-clear way you could see through them and watch other students walking and running down the halls. The teachers and staff at this school, my very favorite, were amazing beyond words. I remember them being so kind and affirming to us, which was a switch from what I was used to.

A memory that rises to the surface of my mind about this school was an event they hosted called a "change challenge" for all the classrooms. The challenge was for the students to bring in change from home, and whichever class gathered the most would win a pizza party. I desperately wanted our class to win, so the next morning while my mom was still asleep—as she always was when I left for school—I emptied all the change from the bottom of her purse. I didn't wake her up to ask because I didn't think she would care. I turned the change in at school, a proud smile on my face. When I got home my mom was furious.

She said, "Jodie, did you take all my cigarette change?" I told her about the change challenge, and when I was done she was fuming with rage. It was all the money we had evidently. My class did win the pizza party, though, so I can't say I wasn't happy about that. It took the edge off having to experience another one of my mother's rages.

That school was a lifeline to me, and I continued there until the end of my third-grade year. It demonstrated to me that there were authentic, kind people in the world, and they patterned to me actions and choices I had not yet seen in my personal childhood experience. A place where families hugged one another, said encouraging words, and protected and nurtured their children. A community that taught me that every child has worth and potential. I would draw from these seeds of kindness and love planted in my heart much later in my future.

CHRISTMAS 1979

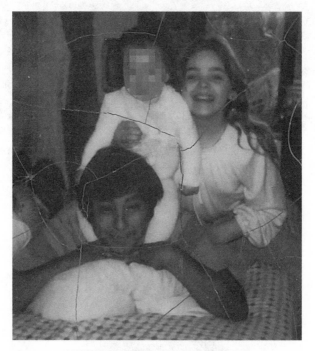

AUSTIN LUCY AND ME JANUARY 1980

JODIE BALLENGER

LUCY SURROUNDED BY BAGS OF MARIJUANA AT THE DRUG HOUSE

PHOTO BOOTH PICTURE OF LUCY AND ME

CHAPTER 5

Kicked out at Eleven

At the end of that summer we moved yet again. I hated to leave this neighborhood and my new school, and I made sure my mom knew it. I grieved the decision she made to move us once again, away from the only place I had ever felt nurtured and safe. A deep anger toward her festered inside me, and perhaps I still have it buried deep in the recesses of my childhood memories. Would we ever settle someplace that was safe, healthy, and kind? Would we always move around like nomads who had to keep on the move to escape the consequences of destructive choices?

We moved to an upstairs apartment that sat on top of a Chinese restaurant. Our house always smelled of lo Mein and fried rice, and I came to associate this smell with this shabby and shadowy place. The apartment was actually nicer than the upstairs apartment we had just moved from, but the neighborhood was quiet and boring—nothing seemed alive and vibrant as it had in the Latino neighborhood.

When fourth grade began, I was intensely disappointed in the school. Situated a few blocks from our house, it was nothing like the amazing school I had left behind. The school was very old and rundown and deteriorating, and the teachers weren't nearly as nice. I was an expert now on moving, though, and tried to adjust to the ups and downs this new place had brought with it. This new apartment was by the Cleveland Metroparks Zoo. I would pass by the zoo and wish desperately that I could go in and see the animals. I learned quickly that those things were no longer for me.

Austin and mom would get into many arguments, many fights. His wife, whom he was still married to, was a Papago Native American as well. They had five children (we got to know them later, enough to call each other brother and sister, but at this point we did not know them). Austin's wife had found out about his cheating with my mother. One day Mom and I pulled up to a house, and Austin's car was there. I could sense by my mom's body language, labored breathing, and narrowed eyes that her rage was seething and about to explode. As usual, I tried to remain quiet and out of her way, praying that it wouldn't be aimed at me.

Mom got out of the car briskly, ripped open a candy bar, and walked up to Austin's car, dropping the candy into his gas tank with a sarcastic smirk on her face. She ran back to our car hastily, and Austin's wife and son came running out the door in a blinding rage. They hopped lickety-split into their car, and a car chase ensued. Mom told me confidently, as Austin's wife chased us, burning up the streets behind us, "Don't worry. Austin never keeps gas in his vehicles." Surprisingly, his wife gave up the chase. I don't know if it was due to the gas or the chocolate in her tank. It turns out Austin and Mom had been arguing, and he'd decided to go back with his wife for a time, which enraged my mother.

Our families were sticky and complicated, and I assumed this must be how all families were. The constant drama, cheating and lying, and violent interactions that kept the children in fight-or-flight mode, never able to relax or feel safe. Our choices affect everyone we profess to love, but all I knew was that Austin was in my life, he had been so kind to me, and I had loved and trusted him. Once again, I was being abandoned, rejected, and discarded. The wall of self-contempt loomed larger and larger with each wounding blow that hit my young mind. The car chase experience left me in a magnified state of inner fear, but my mom clearly wasn't affected and had no concern for how the experience impacted me. She thrived on that type of thing.

Running Away

As stated earlier, my mom was always sick in some way. Whether it was her diabetes, heart issues, or psychological problems, her hospital stays several times a year became a way of life. Not that she really monitored what I was doing when she was home. I pretty much ran the streets and did what I wanted with no supervision or correction. When it looked like she would be going back into the hospital yet again, she decided that my baby sister Lucy and I would go back to Fort Wayne, Indiana, to live with my dad. I didn't want to go back because I was not comfortable with my dad's girlfriend. I had just found a place to seemingly belong, as well as a developing relationship with a boy I met at the skating rink. We talked on the phone all the time, and I was certain I was in love. He even gave me a gold ring to confirm our relationship.

I was out riding a bike with one of my cousins, and we rode to a nearby park. "I can't go back there," I said to her. "I think we should run away. I'm not going to my dad's. His girlfriend hates me. Let's run away together and never look back!"

She thought it was because of how much I loved being in Cleveland, but it was really because of my stepmom and new boyfriend. She knew a boy who might help us, so we hurried breathlessly to his house, which was near Lake Erie. He hid us in a playhouse in his backyard, and he and his brother gave us pickles to eat for dinner because they couldn't sneak any other kind of food out to us! What an odd memory to recall. So, we spent the night in this playhouse, and the next morning we got up and rushed to a gas station to clean up in their restroom. From there I thought if I could only make it to my boyfriend's house, he and his family would surely help me, so we walked all the way to his house, but once we got there his mom let us in and immediately called my mother.

My mom came to pick me up, and instead of giving me a lecture on running away, she took me to the doctor. Mom was certain, with that crazy look in her eye, that I was out having sex and running wild. I was bewildered at her sudden interest in what I was doing—sexually or not. I was petrified as we sat in the stark waiting room, awaiting a probing from a doctor who would say whether I had been sexually active or not. The exam was rough and cold, and soon the doctor came back.

"Yes, ma'am, your daughter is sexually active," he reported coldly, shaming me with his glare. "Her hymen has been broken." I was shocked because I knew I hadn't had "sex" yet, although much touching had taken place over the years from different people. I thought you had to "go all the way" to be having sex. I didn't know how to make her believe it wasn't true. It was a fruitless endeavor to try.

Mom glared at me harshly, and when we left, she said, "I knew you were out looking for boys to have sex with! Always my little stripper girl." I shook my head and insisted, "No, Mom! I have not had intercourse! You must believe me. I'm telling the truth." I was eleven years old.

She didn't believe me, and I wondered about that test—a test that could say what I had done with my body. I thought I hadn't had sex, but lots of different people had put their hands all over my body, inside and out. My mom, who I hadn't told about the abuse, should have been questioning my behavior and why I was so boy crazy and craving their constant attention. She should have observed some of the signs I exhibited that would have tipped her off that I had been molested and abused. But how does someone whose entire life was characterized by molestation, exploitation, and abuse become healthy enough to perceive and discern it in her children? Instead, she was only worried about the act itself. I suspect she may have been worried about my getting pregnant as she did at an early age and the cycle continuing.

We went home, and I knew I would soon be sent back to live with my dad. I have thought so much about that test over the years. When did it happen, what it said I did? I can't make myself remember, though I have tried. I suspect there are still memories buried somewhere deep in the darkest secret corner of my consciousness, the protective walls of amnesia refusing to come down to expose them.

A good relationship can last for many years, through thick and thin, through good times and bad. Others just fizzle and are left lying on the floor like a discarded piece of dirty clothing or a pair of old, worn-out shoes that no longer have any practical use. My parents couldn't live with each other and the cheating, the fighting, and the unbearable truths that severed the last tenuous strings of their marriage.

When the day came for them to go to court again to divorce for the second time, for the strings to be permanently disconnected, the events of that day exposed the truth of the level of dysfunction their entire relationship had endured. Remember the gun my mom had purchased? That gun was calmly and calculatedly slipped inside her purse, and she took my twenty-year-old brother Johnny with her and showed up at the courthouse for the divorce hearing. She didn't care that she was carrying it with illegal intentions. They were going to teach my dad a lesson about what he should or shouldn't be doing. It wasn't discovered on her as they went inside, and the proceedings went smoothly. But when all was said and done and they were all making their way outside—Mom accompanied by Johnny, and Dad with his girlfriend—all hell broke loose.

Dad had discovered that Mom was carrying a gun, after his girlfriend saw it inside her purse. Screaming, name calling, and shouting accusations ensued, and all four of them were having it out on the courthouse steps for all to see and hear. Dad stomped off, realizing this was not the place for this type of altercation to be happening, but Mom and Johnny stalked him in their car, following his every move. They chased him, and just when Dad thought he had lost them, they mysteriously disappeared. The realization came over Dad that they had gone to his house to steal his things, as the divorce had left everything with him. The judge had told Mom in the courtroom that she had gotten what she took the day she left him. Everything left in the house was his. He sped toward home and found them there, trying to break in the back door, intending to take the things she hadn't been awarded, but felt she deserved, in the divorce proceedings.

Dad, always quick to revert to his younger ways, pulled a gun on them just like that. My Mom was in her own obstinate rage as Dad waved the gun around carelessly, angry to the core—spewing raving threats at them. "Just leave!" he bellowed, still pointing the gun at them menacingly. The police showed up in a mass of sirens and swirling lights, and Mom informed them that he had pulled a gun on them, threatening them, and in turn he told the cops that the judge had ruled that everything in the house was to remain with him. Nothing was hers. Mom pressed the issue, arguing that he had actually pointed the gun at her. Finally, Mom and Johnny left, but not before the angry rift of a marriage and life gone wrong had been ripped beyond repair. Dad ended up spending six weekends in jail for pulling the gun on her, even though she had taken a gun with her as well. She had never pulled it.

My dad and his girlfriend, Corinne, eventually got married, and she was now my stepmom. A few months after they were married, Lucy and I were shuttled off to be with them in Fort Wayne. With only a few months left of my fourth-grade year, my dad re-enrolled me at Bloomingdale Elementary, a few blocks from his house. I didn't want to be there. I was freer with my mom to do as I pleased with no accountability, because at Dad's we were under a closer watch. Corrine made it obvious she was not happy we were there. What stays with me the most, even to this day, is what happened several weeks after we went to live with them. I loved my little sister Lucy so much and used to talk to her and play with her. She would smile and laugh back at me with her chubby cheeks and playful grin. Her little face beamed up at me, no matter what was going on around us. She loved me, and I loved her. She had found her way into my heart and brought joy and love to my life.

It was painful to live somewhere that you weren't wanted, but I persisted in trying to make it work. One of the few highlights of my time in Fort Wayne was knowing Lucy would be there when I got home from school, smiling up at me and running into my arms. One dark day I came home, and Lucy wasn't there. I looked for her everywhere and finally asked Corrine, "Where's Lucy?" I felt panicked as Corrine said, "She's gone, Jodie. We gave her to your aunt. She's going to live with her now."

My heart sank like a rock in a bottomless ocean. How do you process this type of information when you're eleven years old? How do you get used to the fact that they had given away your baby sister and she wouldn't be with you anymore? To me it was throwing away someone you loved, and I cried inconsolably. She was gone. As a young girl, you don't think about the hows and whys of caring for children, and Corrine hadn't even wanted me—someone who could care for herself. A toddler is even more work and stress when it doesn't belong to you. My dad, having his name on the birth certificate as her father, had the right to give her away as he saw fit. And that's simply what he did.

I never got over this, and a simmering volcano of anger gathered in my heart toward my father for bending to this woman and giving away my baby sister, whom I loved so deeply.

Once more someone I loved was ripped out from under me, and I was left to put another block on the wall of my identity that spelled out: worthless, unimportant, unlovable, undeserving of love and affection, not worth protection and nurturing. I carried so much guilt and shame from the sexual abuse and felt disposable. I sank deeper into the numb recesses of disengaging from my feelings and emotions and ran to the comfortable place in my mind of isolation and walls of forgetfulness. I didn't want to feel anymore. I didn't want to hurt. I would choose to detach when a threat was near. I would not let them see me cry or bleed.

The summer before my mom left my dad, we all went to a campground, where my future stepmom Corrine (and Dad's mistress, I found out later) and her husband had a camper. I remember having so much fun with them and how kind she was to us. What I hadn't known is that my sister Kelli walked in and saw my dad and her together and knew they were having an affair. Kelli never told Mom. When we left with Mom that next fall, she left her husband for my dad. When they got married, the nice lady at the campground disappeared. There is a stereotype of stepparents not getting along with their stepchildren, and I know that stereotypes don't always remain true. In my case, though, they did. She hated me. I had tried as a child to befriend her, for her to like me. Her kids were already grown, and looking back now I can see that she just wanted my dad to herself, free and clear of any children. She didn't want the daily responsibilities and burdens we represented.

Too Old for Christmas

My mom and dad had always made sure that my sister Adrian and I had wonderful Christmases, despite their fighting. We were Christmas babies. I was born December 22, 1969, one day from being one year younger than Adrian. I remember Mom telling me that for my birthday I could pick one Christmas present from under the tree. I always felt slightly cheated because those were my Christmas presents, not my birthday presents. The Christmas I turned eleven I woke up at Dad's house and went to the living room and stopped in my tracks. It was filled with gifts. I tore into those gifts that morning. It wasn't until later that day that my dad and Corinne sat us down and explained that this would be the very last Christmas we would ever have like this. I looked at them, confused, not really comprehending what he was saying.

"You're too old to have Christmases like this anymore, Jodie," Dad said frankly. We'd always had big Christmases, but when my birthday and Christmas rolled around the next year, when I had just turned twelve, I got a twenty-dollar bill: ten for my birthday and ten for Christmas—and it remained that way until I was eighteen. My resentment grew for my father and this woman he called his wife.

Mom was barely making it in life now, barely bringing in any money. Due to being ill all the time she was put on disability and didn't receive a lot. She took Christmases very hard and would sleep most of the day away in a depressed stupor. I believe looking back now it was because of the disappointment in my face when I woke up to nothing under the tree. She did try and buy one gift and it was usually mascara or makeup of some kind. For several years I was sorely disappointed and would cry. Christmastime and my birthday were not joyous times of year for us; it only highlighted what we knew—we were poor, and our most basic needs were not met. Even having a good meal on Christmas or my birthday was not an option. My mom would be lost in her sadness on those days, and I would go and spend the day with friends. The worst part was going back to school after Christmas break, and all the kids would be wearing their new clothes and talking about what they received. I would simply make things up, but still they knew. My clothes were never new, and I didn't even have the right type of clothing for whatever season it was. I asked myself over and over: Why couldn't my dad see this? I could never understand after they got divorced how he just left us hanging, poor and without our basic needs met. After the divorce, he catered to Corrine's and their animals' every need, while his children were neglected.

If I asked my mom for something I needed, she would tell me to call Dad. But you see I couldn't, wouldn't, call him. After I was no longer living with them, I only saw him a few times a year. I didn't want to see him more than that as I nursed the growing anger toward his neglect and abandonment. When I did go to their house to see him, Corrine would always have huge meals, and I continued to see that even his dogs ate better than I did. He showed care and compassion for them. It made me unbearably sad, because I knew he had the money to help, to buy school clothes we desperately needed, but if he couldn't see me—really see—then I wasn't going to tell him or ask him for anything. It was as obvious as the nose on your face. The span of time I was in school, from fourth grade to eleventh grade, he never did do anything about it.

One day, at the very end of my fourth-grade school year, age eleven, I came home from school, when I was still living with my dad and Corrine. To this day, I don't know what Corrine flew into a rage about. She screamed at me out of nowhere to put all my clothes and things into a garbage bag.

"Get your stuff and sit on the porch and wait for your dad to come home!" she yelled, slamming the door violently behind me as I sat down on the front porch steps in utter confusion and fear. I sat with my face cupped in my hands, waiting for Dad to come home. This was who this woman was. There was no pleasing her. I could not make her like me no matter how hard I tried. I wasn't deserving of her respect, her love, her care, or even her toleration. There were times that she wouldn't speak to my dad or me for days on end, stonewalling us to punish us for offenses she refused to even identify. Whenever her kids came over, she would verbally crucify my mom and me right in front of me. The stabbing words felt like a knife going in and out of my heart, over and over. Whoever said "words will never hurt me" lied or never was subjected to the verbal insults of a woman like this. She wanted a reaction from me; she wanted me to cry and crumble into an inconsolable heap. I can feel the pain as if it were yesterday, the ugly names that tumbled from her lips, the ones she called my mom and me. I knew Dad was being put through hell just by my being there, and he rarely stood up to her to protect me. I dove deeper into that numb cocoon as this excruciating pain tried to kill the last part of emotion that existed in my young heart. *I will not show them the hurt. I will not give them the satisfaction.* The volcano of anger deep within me was erupting and the lava was starting to flow.

I sat out on the steps, thrown out, discarded again, and when he finally arrived home he looked at me with a resigned gaze. He drove me in silence to my mom's apartment and left me there. I had been kicked out, but I was relieved and happy to be out of Corrine's presence. He couldn't protect me from her, *he wouldn't protect me*, and I was glad to be gone. She had put me through hell most days I had been there, and I knew Dad would have peace with her now that I was gone and out of her hair.

Having just moved to Fort Wayne, Indiana, Mom and Austin had settled into a very small one-bedroom apartment along with his son and one of his son's friends, and my sister Adrian, so there was barely enough room for me, but we managed. Adrian and I slept in a tiny area much like a closet with blankets on the floor. It was dismal, but it was where I laid my head and slept. We had been uprooted many times before and always made it somehow. Because Austin was with us it was more bearable, as he was always a beacon of light to me. Having one person in my life that cared about me made a huge difference. My mom, after making such a big deal about finding out whether I was sexually active, had seemed to let that part of it go completely. Her relationship with Austin was volatile; she was always berating him, putting him down. It puzzled me because I knew that she loved him deeply—he was the kindest man she had ever been with. When they arrived in Fort Wayne, Austin couldn't hold down a job. He was an electrician, a good one, but didn't know how to keep jobs. He turned more and more to drinking as the job situation grew worse. But as I've said before, Mom didn't know how to show love. Instead she kept venting her rages, spitting poisonous words to keep us at enough of an emotional distance that she could ensure she wasn't too vulnerable and open to be hurt.

Shocked

In this small slice of my life, in this tiny apartment, was where something sacred got casually taken away from me, something I didn't know I even had the right to keep. A couple of my friends and I were hanging out with a boy from the neighborhood. I really liked him and wanted him to know it. We were all laughing and having a good time. There were no adults around. The boy took my hand, leading me slowly to the bedroom. I felt butterflies in my stomach as we walked inside the room because he was a year or two older than me, and I thought he was so cute. I was boy crazy, so boy crazy! We started making out, and he pulled my pants down and his own. My whole life my mom had told me I was her "little stripper girl" and talked openly, crudely about sex. It set the stage for what was about to happen. He got on top of me and proceeded to have sex with me. I remember feeling I was not emotionally ready for this. I had never gone this far before, that I could consciously remember, and had only experienced inappropriate touching and kissing. It was over within minutes, and he climbed off me and indifferently pulled his pants up. I slipped my own pants on quickly, and we walked out together as if nothing unusual had occurred. I sat down on the couch not knowing what to do or how to react. When I turned to my friend, I realized he was taking my other friend by the hand and leading her into the bedroom just as he had done with me.

Stunned, my whole body turned cold with disbelief. After several minutes, she came out of the room without a word, and he walked over to my other friend and took her by the hand, leading her into the bedroom. I looked at my friend and our eyes met, expressionless and unemotional. When my friend came out of the bedroom, we sat there in awkward silence. After he left, we never discussed what had happened—not once. I believe we were all in shock that he had taken all of us into that bedroom, and we had allowed him to do it. Sexual talk had always been casual in my world, but now it had gone way past kissing and inappropriate touching. I believe that, like my mom, molestation had awakened sensations in my body long before they were meant to be.

I ran the streets of Fort Wayne that summer, swimming at the pool daily, so relieved to be away from Corrine. Then we moved once again, back to Cleveland and into the Euclid low-

income housing projects—and another phase of my life began.

JODIE BALLENGER

CHAPTER 6

Living in the Projects

It was back to Ohio for us and into a roach-infested town-house in the projects of Euclid. I loved that I had an upstairs bedroom, though. While the apartment was dilapidated and dingy, a playground bordered our backyard, so that evened things out—at least in my mind. I was starting my fifth-grade year and really liked the school in Euclid, including my new teacher, Mrs. Peacock. I made two best friends very quickly: Lisa, whose mother passed away that year from cancer, and Theresa, who was Native American. Her father, too, passed away that same year.

I loved Theresa's mom, and I realize now that it was because she did the things my mom never did. She worked at a diner near the school, and sometimes over lunch break we would walk to the diner. Theresa's mom would buy us hamburgers and french fries. I savored every single bite of it. She was kind and nurturing, the very things I craved from my family and rarely received.

For a girl in the fifth grade, clothes and looks mean a lot. More time is spent in front of the mirror, and hair and makeup become an obsession. At that time, Jordache jeans were the most popular thing to wear, and I wanted a pair like I've never wanted anything before. The moment I realized there would be no Jordache jeans for me was the moment I realized we were poor. It sank into my head like a rock, dropping slowly to the bottom of the ocean.

We lived in a three-unit townhouse building. My mom continued to be in and out of the hospital with her various illnesses, so a neighbor in our unit would take care of us when Mom had to unexpectedly be admitted. I wish I could remember her name and find her, as she was an amazing woman. She and her husband had two children, and she had no arms. She did everything with her feet, which included cooking, laundry, driving, and so much more. She was fascinating to me because she never let her lack of arms hold her back from what she wanted to accomplish. She was an inspiration to me, letting me see that any situation could be overcome. Her inspiration has come back to me at different times in my life. Her example taught me so much about tenacity, overcoming obstacles, and still finding purpose and joy in life.

We lived in a colorful neighborhood, and there were hundreds of apartments here in the projects, filled with just as many colorful people trying to live their lives the best they could. In the unit right next to us there was a lesbian couple. They had two children, a teenage daughter and a younger son whose name I can't recall, probably because he pushed every single button I possessed. Selective memory perhaps? Both ladies were full-time trash collectors, heading out on trash days to glean and sift through the garbage. They would then sell and trade their discovered treasures to make a living. I remember all of us sitting outside on the porch talking most evenings until it got too cold to do so. I learned so many things through these people and the different ways they lived and the habits they displayed.

That year in Euclid we lived in three separate units. The first one was the best, and sometime during the winter we moved into another unit across the way. We carried our belongings into this new unit and promptly fell asleep because we were so exhausted. When we woke up, we found so many roaches crawling everywhere that they very nearly could have carried us away. It was so terrible that my mom threw a hissy fit to our landlord, and we were moved into another unit that sat closest to the main road. It was also a bit closer to my friends, so I liked it. We still had roaches, but not nearly as many, so we settled in.

We were at our poorest here in Euclid, my mom continuing her gambling addictions. She would be gone all hours of the night playing bingo at the local halls. One night she came home late. I had been dead asleep for hours already, having gone to bed with my stomach empty. She woke me up to tell me excitedly that she had won at bingo and bought me a hamburger and french fries with her winnings. I gobbled it right down, in my pajamas in bed in the middle of the night. I was so hungry but really too sleepy to enjoy eating it.

I remember an instance here where my mom sent me to the corner store with a brand-new book of $60 worth of food stamps. I went into the store and purchased whatever items she had needed and made my way home. When I came in the door, Mom asked for the food stamp book. I fumbled in my pocket and to my horror realized it wasn't there. I had lost it. I was so upset, and Mom even more so. That was a tough month for us, as we had very little food to begin with. There were many months where we survived on beans, cornbread, or gravy over bread and lots of fried potatoes.

But at the end of the school year, another move was soon upon us. We were headed to Muncie, Indiana, as my grandpa was suffering from cancer. I would soon discover what being alone really meant.

CHAPTER 7

Shot at Twelve

Muncie was rough and tumble, and it was where we were to be parked for a while. My Papaw had been diagnosed with cancer, and Mom and Austin decided to move in to help Nanny care for him while he was sick. Nanny was also suffering with cancer. It never occurred to me then that Mom never took care of her own kids the way she should, yet she took the initiative to care for her dad. At the time, I didn't know the abuse she had suffered at his hands, but in retrospect I wonder if she wanted his approval after all those years. Did she crave his attention? Feel some kind of unhealthy obligation? Or did she believe the same lie she had taught me, that no matter what family did to you, you put up with it because after all they are family? I didn't question it but soon found out that my sister Adrian and I would be living separately from them. In fact, we would be living across town—in our own tiny trailer.

Situated on an angled corner lot in Shed Town, this little trailer was nearly one-fourth the size of a normal one. It sat haphazardly, with other larger trailers. They paid for the rent, and I'm sure they didn't tell the owners that twelve- and thirteen-year-old girls would be living there alone without any supervision. We were one block away from an aunt and uncle's home, and they were to check in on us from time to time.

I remember cooking our own meals in the teeny-tiny kitchen. The bedroom was so small you could barely turn around in it, let alone sleep. We lived off pork fritters from the local store, five for fifty cents, and they satisfied the hunger that crept up on us from not eating properly. A relative taught me to walk into a store with no money and steal candy. Quickly they would go into our pockets, and we would scramble out the door, popping them in our mouths to satisfy the chocolate cravings and make our bellies feel full. I also learned to scavenge for pop bottles and turn them in for money, which could be very lucrative if I could get a nice amount of them.

I had a mouth like a sailor, always trying to act older than I really was. I wanted to look and sound mature, yes, but I realize now that I sounded like a little girl who was raised around unsavory folk who had nasty mouths, vulgarly chattering on about sexual things believing those things were funny. I felt mature because I'd been smoking marijuana and taking pills since I was nine. I thought I had earned my street credit, but I was still a little girl who didn't have direction or purpose. I craved attention and wanted desperately for people to notice me.

We lived in that small trailer for a month or two before my mom moved us to a small house on Twelfth & Gharky. We weren't alone every moment in this house, but we were on our own a lot. Mom and Austin were still taking care of grandpa at this point, and when we moved into this house, we realized that we really were on our own; the task of taking care of Papaw took priority over raising us or meeting our needs. We were responsible for making sure our stomachs were full, whether it was fair or not. Twelfth Street was a main thoroughfare through Muncie, with lots of traffic that traveled by our house. Sitting outside on the porch, watching traffic and people go by, we met a lot of kids from the neighborhood. I had my friends, and my sister Adrian had her friends, who were in and out of the house like a pack of animals. With no parents around, no supervision or rules or guidelines, what could be better?

A pivotal event occurred in this house that will always stay with me. Adrian had several friends over, and they were all packed inside the house mingling and laughing. My friends and I were outside on the porch, and I decided I wanted to go inside. I pushed on the door but was met with someone shoving the door back at me. They wouldn't let me in. I pushed even harder and met with more resistance. I began to get agitated and angry, that they wouldn't let me in when the door suddenly swung open and there stood a guy friend of my sister's glaring at me. He was perhaps a year or two older than me, but the look of disgust on his face was chilling.

"If you try to come in here, I'm going to shoot you," he threatened, waving a gun in the air, pointing it toward my face. *There's no way he's going to shoot me*, I thought stubbornly as I tried to push past him, but suddenly he fired the gun inches from my face.

I was stunned and slipped instantly into shock, hearing my own screams distantly as if they belonged to someone else. I couldn't see. I bent over in agony; I was in so much pain. Realizing it was a tear gas gun, it looked like a real gun in every way. My skin was on fire as the tear gas spread over my face and into every crevice. Blinded by the burning gas, my sister and our friends panicked. I heard them debating whether to call an ambulance but decided not to because there were no adults there and they were afraid they would get in trouble.

"We can't let anyone find out we are home alone because they'll take us away!" I objected hysterically. Imagine making a decision at age twelve, that you don't want an ambulance to come when you're in desperate need, so they wouldn't find out how you're living. My entire face felt as if it were melting off. They brought me wet towels and held them gently to my face, as mucus dripped from my nose and mouth. All the while I felt as if I were choking to death. After what felt like an eternity, I slowly lifted a corner of my eye to discover whether I could still see. I was terrified I would be blind for life. Finally, my sight returned, and my sister and I breathed a sigh of relief.

Boys were always in the picture, and at twelve years old I continued down the path of sensual relationships that had begun for me at such a young age. Once school started, I began dating a guy who was in the eighth grade who was a couple years older than me, and we would get high and have sex regularly. After having sex with him I would cry and didn't know why. I felt an overwhelming wave of sadness and emptiness. Looking back, I realize I was too young for the emotions that being sexually active brought.

The kids who lived at the Children's Home were sent to Wilson Middle School, and my elementary school sat right beside Wilson. Students would gather in the morning to smoke before class in an alley across from the school. As a sixth grader, I would go to this alley to meet with friends and have a smoke before school. A relative of mine was there, and she was upset that her boyfriend was cheating on her. She was in the Children's Home and could not get into any more trouble, so she asked me to beat this girl up. I told her I would, and about that time the girl in question walked by the alley. I walked right up to her and punched her in the face. She dropped to the sidewalk instantly. Rage filled me, and I pounded her in the face, hit after hit, until blood was everywhere.

She got up and ran toward the door of the school. Other kids gathered in a frenzy as she desperately pounded on the door to be let in, her bloody handprints clinging there. Finally, someone opened the door and she ran inside. When the principal arrived to investigate what was going on, I had already slipped away and over to my own elementary school. It wasn't long before I was pulled out of class by my principal and questioned about the altercation. Of course, I denied it vehemently and got away with it. The volcano of anger in me had erupted with furious lava as the result of twelve years of neglect, abuse, and riotous living. It was flowing in a steady, hot stream now, and it would burn anyone who came close to it. No one dared to mess with me anymore. I made sure of it.

Crazy drama was always going on at my house, and I remember two runaway brothers, several years older than me, that Adrian and I allowed to stay at the house. I believe I remember them so well because we fed them bologna, mustard, and cheese sandwiches. We didn't have a lot of food, but we had a lot of bologna and cheese. They stayed several days, and I never saw them again. I also cannot eat bologna, mustard, and cheese sandwiches to this day. I had enough of them to last me a lifetime.

Christmas Cake Fiasco

My sixth-grade class was having a party, and I wanted to make something for it. I signed up and marked that I would bring a Christmas cake. I asked my mom for ingredients, and she did buy those for me, but I was on my own as far as making the cake. Home alone, I laid out the ingredients and began to mix them carefully. I wanted the cake to be just right. I went to the oven after the cake mix was in the pan and discovered it wasn't hot although I had turned it on. I remembered that our stove was broken, and I would need to light the pilot to bake it. I found a piece of paper, rolled it up, set it on fire from the burner, and opened the oven again to light the pilot light. *KABOOM!* The gas had already been turned on for a bit, and when I leaned in with the burning paper it was as if the air caught fire! The gas that had been escaping from the time I turned it on blew up with a startling explosion. The hair on my arms, as well as my eyelashes and eyebrows, were singed off. I was lucky the house didn't explode!

I collected my bravery and bullish tenacity, because this cake was going to get baked one way or another. Calming my racing heart, I returned to light the pilot, this time doing it the correct way, and after thirty minutes I had baked the cake. I placed it carefully on a bare piece of cardboard cut to look like a platter—that's all I had to carry it on—and carried it proudly to school. When I arrived at school, I placed my cake next to the others on the table. As I looked around and saw all the festive things other kids brought in, placed on beautiful dishes, I was embarrassed by my brown cardboard platter. It always seemed, no matter how hard I tried, it was never good enough or met the standards of everyone else. These kinds of moments continued to chip away at the foundation of my self-worth, convincing me I was no good, of no value, and never would be.

At some point after Christmas vacation both my sister Adrian and I were sent to the Children's Home. I can't remember the specifics of why. They called my mom to bring in some clothes for us. She brought dirty underwear, our names written on them in ink, placed inside a tattered brown paper bag. I was mortified, the embarrassment searing my heart like a hot iron. Just another confirmation that she did not know how to be a true mother, although I loved her anyway. The Children's Home bought us new clothing because we had none. I was thrilled to get new clothes, but I couldn't understand how my mom could have done that to us. Had she done it knowing they would buy us new things? Or was she in one of her manic modes where nothing made sense? You can't make sense of an unsound mind, and my trying to find the logic in many of her actions and decisions was a fruitless venture. I didn't care once I had new clothes in hand, because previously I wore old hand-me-downs.

We had cousins that lived not far from us, in the house on Twelfth Street, and their mom, my dad's first cousin's wife (who I called my aunt), shared the same name as my mom: Judy. Aunt Judy was tall and had long strawberry-red hair with lots of freckles. She was a shy, quiet, and peaceful woman who loved her three daughters. She was married to my Uncle Bucky, who was a horribly abusive, narcissistic man. She and her three girls suffered from both mental and physical abuse at his hands. I enjoyed hanging out with them. Uncle Bucky was a truck driver but never did much for, or with, his family. They never had enough, and it wasn't because he didn't have it, but that he kept it for himself to spend on other women when he was on the road. He left his wife and three daughters to basically fend for themselves with barely enough to survive. I didn't like to go over to their house, which stood four blocks from my house, when he was home. He was a hateful, cruel man to his family but was the nicest man to me and others.

Dumpster Diving

One time Aunt Judy came over when Mom was home and not with my grandparents and asked her for a ride to Uncle Bucky's work so she could pick up his check. We all piled into my mom's car and drove over to his workplace and waited for Judy to come back. When the car door opened, her beautiful hair was swirling around an angry, hurt face. She held up a check that contained the amount of one cent. He had drawn all the money out while he was on the road womanizing, leaving his family with nothing to live on. Unlike my mom, Aunt Judy was ineligible to receive government assistance because her husband made too much money. I can still see her crying, her head hung low in hopelessness, not knowing how she would feed her kids. I saw my mom put her head against Judy's and say, "Judy, we will figure out a way..." In that moment I saw a glimpse of the mother I knew my mom could be.

Later, I saw a plan that was hatched, one of desperation and the will to make sure your family didn't starve. They lived across from a fresh produce stand, and one evening when it was dark, the plan was relayed to us clearly through my mom and Aunt Judy: we ran across the street and went dumpster-diving in their trash bin. I recall feeling determined to help her any way I could after witnessing her weep in such despair.

There were still perfectly good cabbages, peppers, and more that was edible and wholesome for hungry tummies. We loaded our arms full of food excitedly and ran back across the street, women helping other women. She endured many years of abuse, which always made me sad, but she eventually divorced him after finding more evidence that he was using their money to shower other women with gifts and provisions on his many trucking jobs.

My Papaw passed away in February 1983 at age sixty-six, and my Nanny died from lung cancer in May of that same year, at fifty-six. She had half of one lung left. An abuser leaves an imprint on you that is hard to break away from, and even at the very end of his life, my mom couldn't seem to pull away from my Papaw, who had molested her for so many years. Mom returned home full-time after my grandparents' deaths because there was no other place for her to be now. As soon as she came back, she and Austin had one of their many falling outs. Shortly after her return, Mom tried to take her life by an overdose of pills, the grief overwhelming her like a mysterious, dark fog. I personally think she was bipolar, as well as in a constant state of survival. Your heart can become sick from so much hope deferred.

One time, out of a handful of times, Mom was admitted to the psych ward and we were sent to live temporarily with my

Aunt Brenda and Uncle David. That year, she wasn't really with us even when she was home; she seemed very distant and detached. We were used to running wild whether she was home or not, and it didn't stop us from doing what we wanted. Mom had mentally and emotionally checked out, and we were left to pick up the pieces. She would pay no mind to us, leaving us no choice but to raise ourselves, and then suddenly switch gears, change the rules, and want to enforce guidelines that were never kept before. This contradiction only added to our issues and confrontations. She would beat us unmercifully for something we had been doing for months, but suddenly she would fly into a rage and tell us it was forbidden. The constant, inconsistent changing of rules and boundaries leaves a child never knowing what is truly right or wrong, or what is permitted or not, and pushes them to exasperation. There was no way to win with her or make her happy because the rules changed so rapidly back and forth that we felt like we were running in circles simply chasing our tails.

It was like being in a tunnel and at both ends a murky swamp of torture awaited, and either way we ran we would wind up in agony—a serious double bind. Mom never attempted to teach us about personal hygiene, to tell us to shower, brush our teeth, or apply deodorant. We didn't have sanitary pads when our time of the month came and had to use toilet paper. We didn't have the benefit of our basic needs being met or of the usual instruction and training most children get from their mothers. She did keep us supplied in cigarettes, allowing us to smoke in front of her at a very young age. It was an upside-down time of confusion and chaos.

I was running amok in my young life, smoking both cigarettes and pot, taking pills, and having sex. Aunt Brenda and Uncle David knew we had a major lack of supervision, and it was forcing us to live like we were grown-ups, getting into all kinds of trouble and dangerous situations. My aunt and uncle knew a detective and wanted to scare me a bit into straightening up, so they took me to the juvenile detention center, and that is where I was introduced to Detective Logan.

"If you don't set your life straight, you're going to end up here, Jodie," he said kindly. "You don't want to be here." I do wish I had listened, but at the time I knew that I wouldn't. My life was hell-bent on running hard in the streets and searching for the love I never had or felt. I was on a relentless journey to fill the empty void in my soul, devoid of self-worth, purpose, or healthy direction. The detective would play a role to come in the happenings of my life, but as a twelve-year-old, I couldn't see past the end of the day, let alone the years to come.

At thirteen now, my boyfriend at the time decided to break up with me to see another girl. It didn't sit well with me, and I found out who she was. It didn't take long for me to find her walking down the street one day. I said, "Are you Brandy?" She nodded yes, and I lunged for her, not even hesitating. She had no clue why I pounced on her! I beat her up with my fists and drew blood, drinking in the damage I was doing. It gave me a kind of twisted satisfaction. I left her bleeding and crying as she stumbled away in pain. I walked away feeling like some of the lava flowing from that volcano of anger had found a small outlet. It felt good. I moved on from that boy and never looked back. I was a fighter, and most would agree that I could fight just as hard as any boy could. I wouldn't let anyone have one over on me. Never. Even if it meant using my fists. If I could not control the crazy, unpredictable insanity of my family life, I would at least make sure I would not be bullied at school. I developed a reputation for being tough and mean, and I enjoyed that reputation.

Also, in sixth grade, I met a girl named Lisa and we became fast friends. She was two grades ahead of me. I skipped weeks of school while hanging out with her and her sister at their house. When I did attend, I really loved my sixth-grade teacher, Mr. Wagner. He was kind to me and noticed the situation I was in. He saw that I was embarrassed when I brought my cake on the cardboard platter. He went out of his way to compliment my cake and help me feel better.

When my mom and dad divorced, my dad was on unemployment and ordered to pay thirty dollars a week per child, which isn't a lot. He was without work for about a year and went back to work and made good money, about five hundred dollars or more a week, not counting side jobs that earned him hundreds more per month. This was in the 1980s, so he was making really good money. My mom never took him back to court to raise child support to what it should have been, so we could have the things we so desperately needed like clothes for each season, shampoo, deodorant, the normal things that most people wouldn't even think about because it is a given that you would automatically get these things for your children. In his mind he was doing exactly what he was ordered to do: pay the thirty dollars per week and nothing more. I never understood how he could come and visit us and not see that we were in desperate need of basic things and not do anything about it. When I would tell my mom I needed clothes or anything else, she always told me to call my dad, but I couldn't do it.

We were so poor we used dish soap for everything, to wash our hair as well as our clothing, which we would ring out in the tub and hang to dry. I would iron my clothes to try and get the wrinkles out, but they were still so wrinkled, and I felt everyone staring at me when I walked into class with my clothes never as clean as they should have been. One day I decided to write a note to say I needed to be dismissed from school just before lunch to go to the doctor. I signed it as my mom and showed it to Mr. Wagner. I think he knew that I had written it, but he sent me to the principal's office for me to show him, and surprisingly they let me leave. I was never sure how that happened. Mr. Wagner noticed my hurt and pain, picked up on what was behind my misbehavior, and had compassion despite what my attitude showed.

Lisa and I had lots of adventures, some not as smart as others. We once decided that we were going to run away from home with a boy we knew. The three of us packed a small bag each and started walking toward the highway. It got dark outside, so we decided to spend the night in the woods. We laid down on the ground of the woods across from Southside High School, trying to get comfortable. It was in the early fall, but this night was extremely cold, and we had nothing but our small bag, and we were miserable. There was no getting comfortable. It was so cold that night that we nearly froze. We woke up and trudged across the woods to a stranger's house that was close by. The night was so horrible we just wanted to find some warmth and comfort. A lady answered the door, and we asked if we could use her phone. We called Lisa's sister's friend Susie and asked her to pick us up and drive us to the highway. As we were waiting on Susie to show up, the lady pulled out weed and offered to smoke a joint with us. She told us later that her husband was a teacher at the high school. I was so shocked to think that a teacher's wife would have this mentality and smoke pot with us. I was always meeting eccentric people who took me by surprise. Susie picked us up, and we thought she was going to drop us off at the highway as we discussed in the car, but instead she told us she had to run an errand first and then took us straight to my house—and my mom was there.

My mom was upset. She took me right over to juvie and left me there. I don't believe I was there for long, but I was put on probation for this incident. When my mom took me to juvenile detention, it was at the end of the school year and close to sixth-grade graduation. When my teacher, Mr. Wagner, looking back, was my favorite teacher to this day. When he came to see me in juvie, he told me he had asked if I could attend six grade graduation. They told him I could if I wore handcuffs. He said we could put a jacket or sweater over the handcuffs so that no one would know. I told him I wouldn't, couldn't, do that. The fact that he took the time to even do this touched my heart and made me think he must have really cared about me. However, that was the last time I remember seeing Mr. Wagner, and it made my heart burn with sadness because he was the best teacher I had ever had and one of the few adults who showed compassion and kindness to me at this juncture of my young life. I would look back on his kindness in the future as an example to me that there are good people in the world and as a pattern on how to show true kindness.

There were moments when we were on our own that Mom would do something she thought was the right thing to do. Do you remember Lisa's sister's friend Susie? We called her Susie Q, the one who had picked us up from the woods. She was a big girl with long, stringy, midnight black hair, dyed within an inch of her life. She was goth before I had even heard of goth and was obnoxiously loud in a way that made you want to retreat from her presence. For those who don't know that term, she sported black hair, black clothes, thick black eyeliner, and her white skin was a stark contrast to the blackness of everything else. None of us liked her, but she had a car, and we had no one else to depend on. Mom had met her several times and asked her if she would stay with us while she was away. What mom didn't know was that Susie was psycho. She was a pot-smoking, irresponsible, uncaring psycho! Mom never could discern people or their character.

A good friend is hard to find when you're living in a world that is cruel to you. Trust was an issue for me, and I didn't have much of that to spread around. I had met Lisa that spring. It seemed we brought out the very worst in one another, instigating each other to destructive choices, goading one another on in a way that was almost addictive, contagious.

Truth be told, our backgrounds were so similar and our soul wounds so parallel it was like seeing your reflection in the mirror. Neither of us had anything within us at that time to encourage the other to rise higher or make wiser choices. Lisa's mom was never home because she took care of Lisa's sick grandma, just like with my mom. That meant the house was empty most of the time. Her place was the party house on the corner, and it was partially my refuge from going home.

Lisa and I once beat up a friend named Kalani simply because we wanted to. It was Lisa's suggestion, and I decided to go along with it. I'm not sure now of the reason, but it probably had to do with a boy. Lisa wanted me to go upstairs and lure her down to her driveway. I felt some hesitation about what I was about to do, a stab of conscience, but I had to stay cool with Lisa. Where Lisa would lead, I would follow. Yet I was the one always in trouble with the law.

I knocked on Kalani's door pretending I wanted to hang out with her, and she naively followed me downstairs as we laughed and chattered. When we arrived at the street by her driveway, Lisa stepped out from behind a car, her mouth twisted into a cocky smirk. I didn't know what Lisa's beef was with Kalani, but it was immediately evident that something was going on between them as a look of dread evaporated the smile on Kalani's face. Lisa began pummeling her in the face with her fists. I stood by watching until we left her crying on the ground, bruised and battered. I kicked her as Lisa and I ran away to escape being discovered by the law or nosy neighbors. I remember feeling horrible after this incident. Later Kalani's mom pressed charges against us. We had to go to court with our mothers, where we were both given community service.

Lisa and I became even closer during our community service. I did part of my community service at the YWCA, and from there they sent me to the animal shelter where I would clean out the cages and do whatever they instructed me to do. It was supposed to be a punishment after all, but I was so excited because I loved the idea of being around animals. I remember, the second week I worked there, a man asking me to come into a separate room to help him. "Sure!" I said nonchalantly. He handed me a cute, fluffy white cat once in the room, and then he asked me to hold him still in my arms while he gave the cat a shot. Almost instantly the cat began to make strange, crackling noises that I later learned was a death rattle.

Oh my gosh! He's killing this cat! I thought with alarm. I wanted desperately to drop the cat and run, but I stayed. The cat went limp in my arms, death having come quicker than I had time to absorb it. He took the cat casually from me, and I numbly walked out and hurried home feeling traumatized.

When my probation officer asked me how community service went, I told her what happened. I figured it was all part of the job and that I had no choice but to obey what he asked me to do. "You did WHAT?!" she exclaimed in indignation. "You do NOT have to do that!" I was never asked to do that again.

We partied a lot that summer after sixth grade, Lisa and me. What kid my age could do whatever they wanted, with no real guidance or boundaries, as if they were eighteen or older? Lisa's cousin and I, at that time, were boyfriend and girlfriend. I was doing as I pleased. One time, Lisa and I went over to her friend's house to hang out. Her friend and another girl there were showing off and revealed to us a whole mess of jeans they had stolen from the mall that day. My eyes widened at the stash. There must have been fifteen pairs of jeans! After we were done oohing and ahhing over their loot, we decided that we wanted to head over to Herbie's Hideaway. Herbie's was a dance place where teens and adults could safely go to dance. Lisa came up with a plan. After we had entered Herbie's we slipped away and back to her friend's house, where we promptly stole the entire lot of brand-new jeans they had scored. We spent the night at her aunt's house that night, and the girls had found out what we did. They showed up at Lisa's aunt's, but she was having none of it and wouldn't allow them in the door. They asked us to come outside, but Lisa's aunt said, "No way! And you need to leave our property now!" She sent them away, and Lisa's aunt kept all the jeans. I never saw those jeans again or knew what happened to them.

Through all the escapades and run-ins with the law, my acts had caught up with me again, and I was once more in trouble with the law because of truancy (skipping school), defaulting on community service, and the altercation with Kalani. I was still on probation, so they sent me to the Children's Home for a second time. I was very upset to be in there but looking back it was a good thing for me. While I was in the home, I was upset that Mom and Austin were still fighting, even to the point that she sent someone to rough him up. I didn't understand my mom and her tactics. To no one's surprise, they split up yet again. I was upset that Austin had left but understood. Mom did live close, so I was allowed some overnighters while I was in the Children's Home.

When I got out of the Children's Home, I was thirteen and in the seventh grade. My mom had moved to Walnut and 9th Street, into a one-bedroom apartment. Our landlord lived across the alley from us and he had an eighteen-year-old stepson named David that I soon had my eye on. He lived across town from us with his older brother, and before long I was hanging out with him. Since I had gotten out of the Children's Home, Mom was trying to keep a closer eye on me by staying at home more and having a few more boundaries, like not staying out all night. She didn't seem to mind that I was hanging out with a much older guy, and again I did whatever I wanted for the most part. I decided it was too late to change the rules now.

It was an oppressively heavy time for my mom with the loss of her parents. Recently two relatives and one of their boyfriends had stolen her car and made it all the way to Texas. They had no money and had stolen food and gas the entire way. When the police put out a roadblock, they ran through it, destroying a police car as well as my mom's car. Now mom had no money, no car, and no boyfriend, as Austin was gone. Since the sixth grade my sister Adrian and I were always in trouble. When I was incarcerated, she was out and vice versa. We were rarely out of trouble at the same time. When I came back from the Children's Home, Austin had left, so it was just my mom and me. When we lived in Cleveland, I know my mom started smoking pot and drinking, but when I came home this time, she was getting high in front of me openly. I can remember coming home once to find her and a friend smoking a bong in the living room. For some people, partying is all about drinking and for others it's pills, but my thing was smoking pot and getting high. One time I got so high I thought I was going to die because my heart was racing uncontrollably. The only thing I could think of to do was to take an ice-cold shower. This seemed to calm my heart rate down and helped me realize I was going to live. One side effect from pot is paranoia. These drug-fueled incidences are hazy pieces of my memory that are difficult to recall in detail.

A woman who lived above us was a prostitute. I didn't know about my mom's years as a prostitute at this time, but one day I came home, and Mom wasn't there. I didn't give it a second thought until my mom, the prostitute, and two men walked down the stairs from her apartment. I gave her a surprised look, but we never talked about it. One night I pushed it too far with her, as I lied and told her I was going to stay with a friend overnight, but I stayed with my boyfriend, David, instead. Her fury overcame her, and she turned me into juvenile detention. I was eventually sent back to the Children's Home yet again.

Scared Straight

While I was in juvenile, a group of girls and I were told that we were taking a field trip. We were taken to the Indiana Women's prison near downtown Indianapolis. We were told that we were taking a field trip, and regardless of the fact that I was in detention myself, I was intrigued by prison. I had never heard of the program called Scared Straight but believe this was the beginning of the program. I had never seen or heard of anything about it. So we had no idea what we were walking into. Scared Straight is a program meant to deter juveniles from a life of crime, showing them firsthand the scariest side of prison so they will be so terrified at what they see that they change their choices. It was very effective. I was excited to be going on this field trip, but as the gates closed behind our van as we entered the women's prison, an eerie feeling came over me.

Once we entered the prison we were taken to the chapel, on the far side of the campus. They fed us lunch, and on each of our trays was placed an orange. Most of us didn't eat much of our lunch because, well, seeing a gate close behind you at a prison will make you lose your appetite. We were in prison! When we were done eating, we threw away everything on our plates - including the oranges. They led us to a group of chairs where we sat down and waited, unsure of what was to happen next. Four very rough female inmates entered the room and introduced themselves. And then chaos erupted. The trash bin was dragged over, and they dug angrily through it, pulling out the oranges we had not eaten.

"Why did you throw these away? What's the matter with you? We don't get no fruit in here! I am in here for murdering someone! I am here for one hundred years, and I don't get fruit, and you throw it away?" They ranted, all four of them screaming over each other in a frenzy, nose to nose with us, spit flying in our faces. They berated us for our selfishness and waste as curses and shouts echoed in the bleak room. We all sat frozen, in total shock, petrified at the verbal assault. All the inmates attacking us verbally were serving very long sentences. They looked us in the eye and emphasized over and over how they wished they had listened to their parents, and how if they had they may not be living out the rest of their lives in prison. Their hot breath scorched our faces as they labored their points, and I remember one woman in particular.

"I'm gonna be on the lookout for you," she said, "watching every face that comes through that door, and I will remember your pretty little faces and come after you! You will be MINE if you mess up and end up here!" she bellowed. I'm pretty sure we all knew what she was saying. I was scared out of my mind, along with all the other girls with me that day. This went on for close to two hours. I glanced frantically at the guards, and they just stood there casually watching. It was obvious they weren't going to rescue us. My heart sank at this realization. None of us had a clue this whole scenario had been staged. It was a traumatic experience I will never forget. I've never been so happy and relieved to leave a place, and when we left, we all said we would never, ever end up in prison like those women were.

CHAPTER 8

My First Love: Danny Lee

The inside of the Children's Home was not scenery I particularly wanted to see again, yet I found myself there once more. The large white brick house loomed against the skyline imposingly. Because it was more like a home than a detention center, it had its redeeming qualities. The front door opened into a reception office, and off to the left was another office. As you walked through the reception area the next room was spacious with a couch, table, and lots of bookshelves that lined the walls. There was another office to the left of the entrance to that room. Stepping out of that room you came to a hallway with stairs leading up to two dorms: the first one for younger teen girls and the next for older teen girls. Downstairs, off a hallway to the left, was a large rec room with a pool table and a stairway that led up to the guys' dorm.

Just off the library, after the stairs leading to the girls' dorms, two large doors led into the dining room. It was the biggest room in the house, with tables for the younger kids and for each of the girl dorms, as well as the guy dorm. Off the dining room to the left was the kitchen. I so loved working in the kitchen with the staff. They were like mothers and grandmothers who were truly interested in me and what I had to say. It felt like they really cared. I can't say that I hated it there because it was more like a home to me than my own. I felt safe there. Something in me knew that the structure and accountability at the Children's Home was good for me. A war raged inside me to feed the addiction of rebellious, destructive living, yet a deeper soul cry sought the structure, guidelines, and nurture I always experienced at the Children's Home. A part of me loved being there.

When I was sent there again, it was close to Christmas. I was the only child at the home who did not get to go home until Christmas morning, only to return that evening. Workers at the home tried to make it special for me and took me to the movies. They were very kind, and I appreciated their efforts, but the only place I wanted to be was home with my mom and boyfriend. Christmas morning, Mom, David (my boyfriend), and his mom, Sharon, came to pick me up. I was so excited to be home with them, and David made sure I had presents to open that Christmas. They were also able to visit me on my fourteenth birthday, several days before Christmas. I'm pretty sure my mom told the home that David was my cousin so he could come visit me.

A few weeks after Christmas I broke up with David. He was an extremely nice guy who wanted to take care of me and treated me well. The truth is, like my mother, I wanted a "bad boy." He wasn't bad enough for me. What drives one to crave the bad boys? I have since realized that if you think you are worthless and of no value, you don't know how to accept the affection of someone who treats you well, and you don't think you deserve it. You are magnetically pulled to relationships that are unhealthy, abusive, and toxic. Also, you get comfortable with the environment you were raised in and what feels "normal" to you. I thought of other excuses for why I broke off with him, but these are probably the real reasons why.

In January I was asked to be on the committee to help plan for a Valentine's Day dance. This was going to be a big day at the Children's Home. Who doesn't like a party? I was over the moon and so excited to be one of three girls chosen. There were also three guys, making a total of six of us on the planning committee. When we went into the room to start planning for the party, I noticed a gorgeous guy sitting at the table. I found out his name was Danny, and he flirted with me the whole meeting. The next day he asked me to be his girlfriend, which I accepted without hesitation. We were quite the pair after that, passing notes back and forth several times a day, and spending every moment together that we could. I was head over heels for him; he was the love of my life. Young love is nothing if not full of hopeful passion, and we had plenty of it.

Danny was about 5'7, to my 5'3, with a medium build. His long, straight shoulder-length chestnut brown hair made me swoon when it blew in the wind, and his brown eyes were soft and expressive and could hold me captive when he caught my gaze. Amiable and charismatic, magnetically he drew others to him because of his engaging personality. He was a couple years older than me and a guy no one messed with. Soon after we started going together, he got a job at Marsh's Supermarket as a bagger not far from the Children's Home. When the Valentine's dance rolled around, Danny had gotten into trouble—I think for smoking—and wasn't able to attend. I was upset, but what could be done? I invited my friend Jodi from school, and we attended the dance together for fun. One perk to the dance was that they called your name out when your date arrived, and you went out to get them and walked in together. Danny had just arrived back from his job and heard the announcer say, "Jodie, your guest Jodi is here." Danny got upset with me and thought I had invited another boy to the dance. He was upstairs in his dorm upset all night until the other guys got back to the dorm and told him I had not invited a guy; it was a girlfriend. We laughed about it when he told me what he had thought.

Danny grew up in a home that resembled mine and had been able to do whatever he wanted growing up. We connected on that fact alone. I'm sure he probably told me why he had been sent to the home, but I don't remember, and it would not have deterred me from him no matter why he was there. We had recreation time every day. During recreation time on nice days, we were taken outside to bask in the sun. We would sit on the front lawn under a tree and sneak kisses as many times as we could get away with it. He meant the world to me, but our upbringing made certain things seem normal to us that wouldn't have been normal in healthy relationships.

Friends with Benefits

I was able to leave the Children's Home on passes for home visits, for weekends and other special occasions. In June of that year when I went home, a guy I had met at my middle school named Jesse, who was friends with both Danny and me, would come over to hang out. Jesse told me the Muncie fair had started, and he wanted to take me, so Austin drove us—he and my mom were back together, the constant roller coaster of their relationship continuing in its chaos and dysfunction. As we were strolling around the fair taking in the sights, Jesse saw Abby, Danny's sister, and her best friend Mikayla. I had never met his sister, so Jesse introduced us. The moment was awkward, to be sure. Here I am at the fair with a guy that knows Danny and his family, and we run into Danny's sister. My only thoughts were *BUSTED*. This is where the complications began. Growing up the way I had, being a faithful person was something I had never seen lived out in any way, and for Danny it was the same. It would have been great if Danny and I could have been able to take our home passes on the same weekends, but that never happened.

That summer my relationship with Jesse changed. We were what they call nowadays "friends with benefits." Abby bristled when she saw me with Jesse. I knew that when I went back to the Children's Home, I would have to tell Danny. I really wanted to tell him before his sister did. I stayed at my mom's those weekends out, and this weekend with Jesse— and others just like it—were full of sex and drugs. My mom knew everything that was happening and didn't blink an eye. Our upbringing defined toxic practices as normal because it was all we knew. When I returned from the weekend, I got a surprise of my own when my house mom took me aside and gave me some unwelcome news. While being bussed to church that Sunday, Danny sat with and began talking to a girl. She said they were holding hands. It was the very one I had beaten up and gotten in big trouble over. I was devastated, for a moment, that he would do this to me, but my reasoning kicked in and I knew I had just done even worse to him.

This started our unspoken "open relationship." When we were in each other's presence we were together, but both of us knew that when we were away from each other things would happen, and we always excused each other for it. Fooling around with other people happened quite frequently. We didn't like it when it happened and would be upset with each other when we found out, but eventually we got over it and moved on. Our backgrounds didn't allow for normal relationships, and what others deemed wrong we simply excused.

While at the Children's Home we took every opportunity to be together. A friend of Danny's who was in photography at school took our pictures by the swing set, as well as pictures of him pushing me on the swing. We would walk up and down the driveway just talking about everything under the sun. That summer we would lie outside in the back of the home trying to get suntans while we playfully sprayed each other with hoses, me giggling as each of us tried to get the best of the other. I look back on those days as fond memories. I also played on the Children's Home girls' softball team, and how I loved softball! I always played first base. I went to trade school half days that summer and got paid for going. This provided money for me to go school shopping. When we both were released from the Children's Home in July, Danny took me clothes shopping and I got black parachute pants and a black-and-white striped shirt. How I wish I had kept that outfit.

I was released from the Children's Home before Danny and went home to live with my mom, who now lived in Middletown Gardens. It seemed every time I left the Children's Home, I would come home to a brand-new place. Middletown Gardens used to be a military barracks, with neatly laid-out housing that had been turned into government housing, and for us it was a very nice place to live compared to other projects we had lived in. I was happy to have my own room. At the house we had just moved from, my room was a couch in the dining room.

When my mom told me she had moved there I told Danny. He was excited and said he only lived four or five blocks away, and his grandparents lived in that housing as well. When Danny finally got released from the Children's Home a week or two after I was, we discovered his grandparents lived right behind my duplex. Looking out my window, I could see right into the window of his grandparents' place. His grandparents were much older, but I remember really liking them; they were a very musical family. His grandma and grandpa would play the piano and other musical instruments, and people would stop in, and all they talked about was music. We would go to his grandparents' house frequently. Other than that, I was at Danny's house for most of the hours of every day. I basically moved in with him and his family that summer.

Austin and Mom's relationship was back on, and he had recently secured a temporary contract job working in Louisville, Kentucky. My mom wanted to travel with him there to live, where a decent apartment was provided for them. She knew I was basically living with Danny and his family anyway, so she didn't think it was a big deal. She said she would make sure there were cigarettes at the house for me, and off she and Austin went to Louisville. I was happy to be with Danny and his family. By this time, I was used to my mother exiting my life, and I had grown very capable of taking care of myself and not feeling like I needed her to mother me. The deep deficit inside me my parents had created through their neglect and abuse was part of the deep well that watered my destructive lifestyle and my toxic choices.

I loved Danny's mom, Samantha, who seemed like the coolest mom in the world to me. I remember the first time I saw her: It was at the Children's Home; Danny was being picked up for a home visit, and he introduced us. Her hair was buzzed short like a crew-cut with longer bangs, dyed platinum blonde. Always friendly and upbeat, she would go with us to buy pot and smoked it with us on a daily basis. She was the coolest mom, at least in my eyes. Danny's dad was tall and quiet, never having much to say about anything. He was on disability from an accident and sat in his room most days in a haze from the pain medication he was taking. Danny was the second oldest of five brothers and one sister.

Party House

I loved Danny's family and being around them. Their house, hidden behind tall, overgrown bushes, was the party house, and it rocked the corner lot that it sat perched on. You didn't go there to buy drugs; you went there to do the drugs or to drink. Day in and day out, we smoked pot, swallowed pills, and took anything we could get our hands on. His mom did them right along with us. I loved being there with Danny and his family, and I felt right at home. In my teen mind, I still could not appropriately judge that this was not only unhealthy, it was dangerous and abnormal. Danny's mom was more of a party friend. She was aiding and abetting our destruction, but she was on her own path of trouble and devastation.

Those summer days were swelteringly hot, and we would go to the stone quarry that Lisa and I used to enjoy in Shed Town. When you're hot and you don't have money for the city pool, you go where you're able to cool off. One day I showed Danny where the stone quarry was, and he fell in love with it. One hot night we were partying hard and wanted to get pills to keep it going. A friend of Danny's took us to a house to find some, and I proceeded to pop a pill immediately. It was a Valium. It knocked me clean out. I was semiconscious when we got back to Danny's house. His friend asked if they should wake me, and Danny said, "No, just let her sleep in the car." Everything fell quiet as I dropped into a deep sleep in the parked car.

The next thing I knew his friend crawled in the backseat with me. His hands were all over me while I was passed out. Clarity returned and shock set in as I pushed him away with disgust and freed myself from him, running into the house. I told Danny what had happened, and he confronted his friend; it never happened again.

Over that summer Danny taught me how to drive. His truck was a stick shift, which scared me, but Danny assured me I could do it. The very first time he took me out to teach me, we were in a housing addition not far from my house. I was behind the wheel and he was instructing me on all the proper steps. I was concentrating on shifting the gears, and as I looked up we were headed straight into a closed garage door! Thank God, Danny was sitting right beside me and slammed on the brakes and stopped only inches before we hit it. He never let me behind the wheel again.

Party's Over

School started up in the fall. Living with Danny and his family, I would walk to middle school with a couple of his brothers who were both in eighth grade with me. Danny had dropped out of school. I still loved living at Danny's and thought things were going well. I had Danny, I had a family, and it was the way I wanted things to be. One day as I was walking down the street, my Aunt who had adopted my little sister, Lucy, when my dad gave her away, spotted me and decided to confront me.

"Your mom has left town and you're taking care of yourself," she said. "I'm letting your dad know." Before I could stop the next chain of events, my dad was confronting my mom in Kentucky and telling her that he was going to take me to live with him. I was livid, as I did not want to go with him—I wanted to stay with Danny and his family. After supporting my stepmother, Corrine, kicking me out four years earlier, and casually giving away Lucy, allowing me to live the way I had lived, never having much, I couldn't understand why he was so upset about my circumstances now.

I grudgingly returned to the apartment in Middletown Gardens, and my dad came to pick me up with Corrine and take me back to their home. Corrine never allowed my father to be anywhere near me without her being present. Terror struck my heart like a lightning bolt as I thought of living with her again. She had no guard on her mouth, no kind words for me at all. Brutal, cruel words spewed from her mouth freely about my mom. I don't understand how anyone thinks it's acceptable to openly talk about a child's parent in front of the child. It's not okay to do that in any situation, as it will emotionally scar that child. And if this is done in the presence of the other parent, how could they just sit there and allow it to happen? No matter how bad that other parent is, it is still their parent. By the way, both my parents talked crap about each other; it was not one-sided.

I couldn't bear the thought of going back to their home knowing my dad wouldn't stop her verbal and emotional abuse, crucifying my mother and me in front of him. But there I was, making my way back to a home where my stepmother did not want me and despised me. I know my dad thought he was doing what was right, but what he did not understand was that putting me in a home where I had to endure someone who hated me and did not want me there was worse than living with my boyfriend and doing drugs. At least I was wanted at Danny's. Corrine picked right up where she had left off, giving me the cold shoulder, stonewalling me. I felt like I lived in a deep dark hole in the ground where no one could see or talk to me. The oppression smothered me and yet fueled the ever-growing volcano of anger brewing within me, now spewing lava more aggressively into the atmosphere. This volcano was becoming a dangerous threat, and there was nothing I could do to stop it.

Not long after I moved back in with my dad, a court hearing was scheduled to determine my custody. My dad was accusing my mom of negligence, and I was in a state of despair because I didn't want to live with Corrine. For me, it was something out of a cruel fairy tale, the way she treated me, like Cinderella's stepmother. Corrine and I had a bad argument the day before court, for my dad to get custody, so I rushed angrily downstairs to my room. I was in so much despair I no longer wanted to live, and I decided impulsively to kill myself. Horribly distressed and with no place or person to turn to, no lifeline, I felt trapped with no escape except death. I simply couldn't bear this chaotic, torturous life any longer. I fumbled around looking for something to off myself with and decided on a full bottle of Tylenol. I was fourteen and at the end of my rope. I swallowed the whole bottle and lay down on the bed, fully clothed, expecting to never wake up again. I accepted it. I wanted the pain to stop.

Tap. Tap. Tap.

To my surprise, I woke up, groggy from sleep and an excess of pills in my system. I tried to pick my head up from the pillow, but it felt like a heavy rock that I was too weak to lift. It was dark and gloomy outside. I looked up and saw Danny, worried, staring at me through the window, right above my bed. I pulled myself up to the window, and he whispered, "I'm here to get you!" But it was too late. I knew my dad had heard everything, as his bedroom window was directly above mine. I heard him jump out of his bed and head for the front door. I told Danny to leave before he found him. I ran upstairs to try and settle what was going on, having expected to never wake up again. I ran upstairs and outside, and there was my dad, cool as a cucumber, dressed in only his white briefs, with a gun leveled at Brian and Jesse, two friends who came with Danny. I yelled, "Where is Danny?" All this happened as my dad yelled to Corrine to call the police. They told me that Danny had run off down the alley. When the cops rolled up, they sent the other two guys home and never located Danny.

My dad and Corrine were livid. They looked at me screaming, "You knew they were coming! You have your clothes and shoes on, just waiting for them." I looked down and for the first time fully realized that I was still dressed. I couldn't bring myself to tell them it was because I had tried to kill myself. I had no idea Danny was coming to get me. Believe me, if I had I would not have tried to kill myself and I would have been ready and waiting with a suitcase by my side. I was stunned to find myself alive. The custody hearing was held that morning, and when I stepped off the elevator, I found myself looking right at Samantha, Danny's mom, who had come with my mom to the hearing. She told me that Danny had made it home okay.

My dad was awarded full custody of me, with no drama in the courtroom. After it was over, he allowed me to go to lunch with my mom and Samantha. Danny met up with us at the restaurant where I was given the whole story. It turned out that the plan for Danny to come and get me was my mom's idea. She gave gas money to one of Danny's friends to come and try to take me away so dad couldn't get custody of me. I was surprised she went through this trouble to help me escape. Devastated, Danny and I said our goodbyes, and I went back home despondently with my dad.

Once we got back to Fort Wayne, my dad enrolled me in school. One of the first days I began attending Lakeside Middle School, there was a very popular girl sitting next to me in the back of the class. At first she was cordial, asking what my name was, but with a snarky smile she said, "I hear you're going to get jumped today after school." Those words went right through me, as I knew I'd never be able to totally fit in somewhere without trouble. I looked right back at her in belligerent confidence and told her to tell them to bring it on. That they had no idea who they were messing with. She was startled, both at my boldness and my reaction. At lunchtime that day I was invited to sit with her and her friends at the popular table, and with my own snarky smile I said, "No thanks." I found a table to sit at, one with friends I had known from fourth grade. That popular girl was always nice to me from that day forward, as she knew I wouldn't put up with her or tolerate anyone else trying to bully me. I was past middle school drama and had been for a while.

Within the first few days I met an amazing girl named Shelly. She and I constantly wrote notes to each other, hanging out whenever we could. Shelly was a good girl who didn't smoke pot, fight, or party, and I admired her for that. She always talked about going to high school that next year to be on the flag team and wanted me to try out as well. I really liked Shelly and knew she was a true friend. I saw in her life and her choices that you could have fun and not have to drink, do drugs, or fight. Being with Shelly was like a breath of fresh air for me. Once I started hanging out with her, it was obvious to me that she was a better influence on me than my past friendships and that this was what a real friendship, a normal one, should look like. I didn't know I wanted this kind of refreshing, drama-free friendship until I found it in Shelly. Danny was staying in contact with me during this time through phone calls. He assured me he loved me and was waiting for me. For his seventeenth birthday, I bought him an album of the latest and coolest rock band and sent it to him.

She and I loved the song "Purple Rain" from Prince and went to see the movie as soon as it came out. We liked going to the mall and hanging out together. My friendship with Shelly inspired me to want to make things work at my dad's. I wanted to do my best to get on Corinne's good side for my sake, but also for my dad's. I sucked up to her the best I knew how. Some days it felt like it was working and other days it definitely wasn't. After about six weeks of living there, I was over walking on eggshells around her almost every time I was in her presence. I got home from school one day, and she was furious with me. She was doing laundry and found a letter Shelly and I had been passing back and forth to each other. I cussed throughout the letter, and she was angry about the language. I grew up in a home where cuss words were said every other word. I couldn't believe she didn't expect for me to cuss!

That next morning, as I boarded the school bus, all the hell she was putting me through hit me like a ton of bricks and I felt that I could not do this any longer. I was at the end of my ability to endure any more from this woman. I told a friend I was sitting with on the bus about my situation and said I was going to run away; she said she would come with me. The school bus driver was going to be the key, because he had already been eyeing me and making it clear he was interested in me. I always thought he was creepy and a pervert. I asked him if he would let my friend and me off at the next stop. He looked me over and said he couldn't do that, but I knew I could use my feminine wiles to convince him. Batting my eyelashes and whining for a little bit, I let my mouth curve into a sad pout. When he caved, I smiled and sat down with my friend, relishing the victory.

We hopped off at the next stop and snuck back to my dad's house for some money and to pack a few clothes. I knew he had hundreds of dollars in his room, but I loved him and didn't want to steal much. I pocketed ten dollars, left the rest, and wrote Corrine a nasty note on the dry erase board in the hall. I was all about burning bridges back then and didn't hesitate when I wrote it. We ran to my cousin's house where we stayed for two days, then my friend decided to go home. I think she had had enough of the runaway life in two days. I contacted my mom, and she gave my cousin enough money to get me to Danny in Muncie. I had my cousin pull in the alley behind Danny's house. As we turned in, I could see Danny's truck. She parked right behind him, and he was sitting there with another girl beside him. A warm feeling of love for him passed over me, yet I also felt a punch in the gut knowing he was with other girls. I hopped out, and when he saw that it was me, he jumped out of his truck and embraced me, smiling and kissing me, letting me know much he'd missed me. He grabbed my things, and we went into his house. I never said a word about the other girl. He just left her there and went inside. I never saw her again. That was our MO, our method of operation, our unspoken open agreement. It was October of 1984.

Teenage dreams are lofty, full of air and romantic notions. We put our heads together and tried to form a game plan for no one to be able to find us, especially me. We were sure my dad probably called the police and told them I would be at Danny's, so we knew we needed to get away from his house as soon as we could. His dad took us to Indianapolis, where his grandma lived, and we sold her on a sob story of how I was a good girl with good grades and terrible parents. Danny had a friend down the street whose house we went to and got high. His grandma sensed something was off and did not want us to stay. We headed back to Danny's house in Muncie after two days, where we had to come up with another plan. We also stayed with Danny's friend, Roger for a few days. The days melted together in a blur of moving around, sex, drugs, and staying away from being discovered by the cops.

Crystal

One day Danny asked me to come with him. He was selling an end table with a checkerboard on the top. It wasn't unusual to sell things to get what we needed, but this was different. I asked him why he was selling these things and he replied,

"I'm trading it to get high. I like the high that this new stuff gives me. I want you to experience it too!" We walked down the street, maybe four or five blocks, to this itty-bitty house that sat on a side street. We entered the house, and there was an older guy and younger girl there. Danny told the man he wanted to do a couple of lines and wanted me to try a line too. I had never seen this before; it was a line of what looked to be crushed crystals.

"It's called crystal," Danny said as he bent down to sniff both lines up with a flourish. He told them I had never tried it, and soon a line lay waiting for me. I bent my head down, the powder shimmering like diamond dust, and with a rolled-up bill I snorted it in one intake of breath. I threw my head back and waited. An immediate rush of energy caused me to want to go outside and run. I couldn't sit still. I grew restless and jittery as my heart raced, and I had to move. I didn't know these people, so I wasn't comfortable around them, and I told Danny I was going to walk back to his house. I felt like I must pace the floor because I literally could not keep from doing so. The room was tiny, and I didn't want these people watching me. I felt like I was in a movie with cameras filming my every move, a surreal cloud of false reality and delusion as I quickly walked down the sidewalk, the drug coursing through my veins. I had all this nervous energy and felt invincible.

The drug possessed me as I walked briskly in the direction of Danny's house. The sky was brilliant as I was encapsulated in the feelings my drugged mind produced. Off to the side, I vaguely heard a loud car muffler, and it annoyed me like a gnat buzzing in my face. A voice said, "Is your name Jodie?" I turned my head and saw an older man in an older style of car driving at a crawl beside me. I shook my head and gave him the first name that popped into my head, a girl I used to be in the Children's Home with. It slid off my tongue like the many other things I've said in my own defense. He turned the corner, going at a turtle's pace, and I took off at a run as the crystal meth spread through my brain.

I turned down the alley which ran by Danny's driveway, where I could slide right onto Danny's back porch, the overgrown bushes hiding his house from the street. My heart was pounding from a combination of exertion from running and drugs. As I turned into Danny's backyard, I heard the same car's muffler rumbling as it turned the corner of the main street in front of Danny's house onto the side street that ran beside his house. I realized he was probably an undercover detective sent to find me and take me back where I didn't want to go. I flew up the stairs and onto the side porch. I slid on my belly up against the back door and knocked furiously as the car drove by. Danny's mom opened the door, her startled face looking down at me, and pulled me inside.

"It's the cops!" I yelled, hyperventilating at the turn of events, still high as a kite. I knew the car had stopped somewhere outside and the man was looking for me, expecting me to come down the alley. Danny's mom calmed me down as best she could. I took a deep breath to force myself to slow down so she could understand what I was saying. I paced back and forth from their dining room to their living room, hoping Danny would come home soon. Finally, Danny came home, and I told him everything. Suddenly there was a hard knock at the front door. All three of us looked at each other in panic, knowing that no one used the front door except the cops. Danny ran with me to the basement, leaving me there, then ran back up the stairs. My heart was ready to explode, and I paced as I heard doors and muffled voices upstairs. I knew that running away wouldn't end well, but I had to do it. To me, there was no other choice.

My mind sifted through all possible scenarios occurring upstairs, and I couldn't hold still, anxiety riddling my thoughts. Soon, though, I heard Danny coming swiftly down the steps. His face was so gorgeous and dear to me, and there was nothing I wouldn't do for him. I was fourteen and he had just turned seventeen, and I knew in my heart that I loved him.

"Jodie, they know you're here," he said. "They told my mom you have to come out or they will get a warrant, and if they find anything illegal in the house, they'll take the boys away." My mind started spinning; we knew they would find something in the house. And just like that, the house of cards we had built came crashing down. I looked deep into his eyes and knew the running was over. A detective was posted at the front of the house and at the rear; the house was covered. Danny walked me sadly upstairs to the back door. We both knew that after this we wouldn't be seeing each other for a while. I reached up to kiss Danny, my drug-induced haze only lessening slightly, and he kissed me back, his mouth covering mine longingly.

"I'll wait for you," he said. "I'll be here." And with that we walked out of the house. I was handcuffed and put in the backseat of the detective's car. I realized that the detective who slammed the door and looked inside at me was the same man who took me to juvie the first time and tried to scare me out of ever needing to go there. His name was Detective Logan, and he was a good man. His eyes bore into me, and I knew that he cared. He understood I was a lost young girl running away from a troubled home life. I looked out the window, and Danny's house grew smaller in the distance as we headed downtown.

I found myself in the office of Detective Logan where they asked me a few questions that I did not answer. They had to know I was high on something. He told me I'd be heading to court in the morning then ushered me into a tiny cell—high on crystal meth. Later he transported me to juvie, where I'd been in and out since I was eleven years old. I paced the floor of the tiny space inside my cell and finally lay down, succumbing to the cares and stress of the day, the running, and the drugs my body had absorbed.

My eyes opened slowly, adjusting to the steel cot I was sleeping on, trying to remember what happened. The effects of the crystal meth stayed with me, but I could feel my brain settling back to normal, and I knew it had worn off enough for me to think straight once again. I knew the juvie schedule quite well: wake up early to the radio playing, get out of cell, and do some cleaning, take a shower, then go to eat breakfast. I thought it was weird that there was no music playing. I had never been there when the music wasn't playing in the morning as a wake-up routine. Shaking my head to clear the fog, I heard the guard's keys unlocking all the cells. All the inmates lined up to be walked through the morning's regular routines. I proceeded with the set routine then soon found my way en route to court.

When I entered the building, the officer took me to my probation officer's office. On this morning the officer seemed to be rushing me in, his feet moving with determination. As I was being walked by other probation officers' offices, I saw Danny's sister Abby's best friend. She looked at me with anguish on her face.

"Jodie, did you hear what happened to Danny?" she said. In that second, time stood still. A vortex of stalled time signaled to me that I was about to hear something that would shake the very core of my being and pierce through my heart like a sharp sword. I looked at her and shook my head no as they urgently pushed me forward into my probation officer's office, where to my surprise my mom was sitting. She looked at me, her eyes glassy with dread, and I could tell something was radically wrong.

My probation officer said quietly, "Danny was in an accident last night." My eyes went out of focus as I looked at her lips moving, but not comprehending.

"How is he? I want to see him," I answered, fear washing over me like a tidal wave. "I want to see him right now!" I saw her head shaking no, slowly going back and forth, as a dense fog of despair descended over me.

"He didn't make it, Jodie. He died," she said as she handed me a newspaper. Black glaring headlines screamed out words I didn't want to see, a photo of Danny's wrecked truck with men standing around his body. I felt my lungs give way and there was no breath inside of them.

"You're lying! You're not telling the truth!" I sobbed uncontrollably, screaming in agony and grief. I felt myself sinking into the chair as the probation officer and my mom tried to help me understand what had happened. I heard them talking about drinking and a tree and being partially thrown from the truck, and I simply didn't want to hear it, couldn't bear to hear it, as my heart shattered into a million pieces. The reason the radio wasn't on at juvie that morning was because the story was all over the news, and they didn't want me to hear it that way. I tried to focus on what was reported by the newspaper, reading over the details that my mind refused to absorb:

THE MUNCIE STAR // *Thursday November 8, 1984*

Muncie teenager killed in crash; Passengers Hurt

According to county patrolman John Sciscoe, Ruble was driving a pickup truck northbound on Burlington Drive at high speed when he lost control of the truck and struck a utility pole.

Sciscoe said that it was believed that the youth was driving at high speed, and that his mother, who was sitting beside him, turned off the ignition. Ruble, Sciscoe said, turned the ignition back on and "floored it." When he did that, Sciscoe said, the truck zig-zagged several times before finally going off the west side and striking a utility pole on the driver's side. Ruble was partially thrown from the vehicle, he said.

I closed my eyes and let the news wash over me. Danny was gone. I later found out that after I was taken, Danny had started drinking. This on top of the crystal meth and the pot he had already done with me earlier in the day. He was speeding, and his mom had tried to get him to slow down, but he wouldn't listen. The two friends in the truck ran away from the scene of the accident, afraid they would be in trouble for drinking, but his mom stayed with him, sitting there with her injuries as he lay lifeless on the ground.

I couldn't fathom the gravity of what had happened, and I cried until I couldn't cry anymore. I still had my court hearing to attend on top of this trauma, so I was led into the juvenile courtroom where the judge sentenced me back to the Children's Home. You would think the realization of what caused the man I loved to die from choices of drugs, drinking, and speeding would have changed my direction in life and the decisions I would make in the future. But you would be wrong. This volcano of rage inside me had now begun to explode with the complicated grief that was fueling its energy. I was a walking time bomb.

After the hearing, they took pity on me and let me go to Danny's house where all his family was gathered. The feeling inside of me was a mix of grief, shock, disbelief, and denial. Surely Danny would just walk into the room anytime, laughing and hugging me. His mom and dad were there, and I hugged them, feeling their bodies shake with sobs. I was overcome with regret, feeling partly to blame for all of it. They went over the story again, feeling the need to tell it, to let it out. I just cried and knew that if I had stayed with my dad none of this would have happened. But you can't go back and there are no do-overs. Ever. I felt eyes on me, dirty glances that implied blame and fault, and I turned my shoulders to these glances, willing them away. I had loved Danny so much, but we were such young and reckless teenagers, and the choices we made had set a course that escalated toward a finish line of destruction and despair.

As a child of fourteen, I had felt grown-up, yet totally unprepared and not knowing how to control or deal with my emotions at a funeral for the man I loved. The calling hours were held the day before his funeral service and burial, and I attended in a blur of crying and instability. The casket was open, and Danny lay in repose dressed in camo army pants and a green T-shirt. It was something he had worn and felt comfortable in. It seemed right to bury him in this outfit. My mind could not comprehend Danny dressed in an outfit for burial. My mind was racing as day turned into night and I found myself numbly preparing for the funeral of my boyfriend. Danny's casket lay open to the world. The mortician had done the best he could to make him presentable. I was not prepared to see him in the casket, cold and gone from this world. I kissed his forehead as I held his hand. He was cold, as cold as the kiss I planted on his skin. A lot of teenagers attended his funeral—the place was packed. Many condolences floated over my head as I watched them file through and shake hands with his family.

Danny's family was Catholic, and the funeral was an awakening to the strange and different ways of religion. At the Children's Home, they would bus us to different houses of faith: Protestant, Catholic, Lutheran. I had been in Catholic services before but never to a funeral. I wasn't prepared for what it would entail. As they sat me with his family in the huge Catholic church, the rituals and repetitions of this faith were so foreign and unnatural to me. I had gone to church intermittently throughout my youth, and Mom had taken us to only Pentecostal churches, which compared to the Catholic Church was a rollicking good time held in the aisles of small churches. My body wracked with sobs and the tears flowed freely, uncontrollably, as the ritualistic ceremony began. I remember the priest swinging a smoking gold container on a chain over his casket, its meaning lost to me. The funeral continued. As I was lost in my memories and sobbing, I could feel the annoyance of Danny's family spread over me. I was only the girlfriend, and a young one at that.

The church itself seemed strange and unnatural, and I struggled to comprehend that this was Danny's funeral service and after the service he would be buried and I would never, ever see him again. A casket lined with silk, holding the boy I had loved, the only one I felt really loved me. As we left the funeral, the cavernous church seemed to press down on me with its strange symbols and meanings. I couldn't absorb it or accept it, and when we made our way to the cemetery, I found myself longing for the day to end, as what had happened would never be real to me. The cemetery where he would be laid to rest was pretty far away. For the graveside ceremony my emotions were out of control. I sobbed with complete abandon, not caring or even noticing what others might think. I sat beside his family, and I vaguely remember the priest handing me something. I looked up at him, to this day not knowing what he was trying to give me and shook my head no—motioning toward Danny's mom beside me. I realized they had thought I was his wife, as I had always looked older than I really was. I took off my necklace and put it at his gravesite, one last thing I could give him. It was all I had to leave with him to show him my love.

Once the graveside service was over, we went back to the church for a luncheon, and I felt all the blame—a red letter pinned to my shirt—of a family that, just like me, didn't know how to say goodbye or reconcile what had happened.

MUNCIE INDIANA CHILDREN'S HOME 1980'S

ME KELLI ADRIAN LUCY AND MY NIECE KAREN

THANKSGIVING 1983

A FEW MONTHS BEFORE I MET DANNY LEE

ME AND A FRIEND DANCING AT A PARTY AT THE CHILDREN'S HOME

A FRIEND AND ME AT THE CHILDREN'S HOME

DANNY HAD ONE OF HIS FRIENDS TAKE PICTURES OF US AT

THE CHILDREN'S HOME

DANNY AND I AT HIS HOME

On the Run and Living with a Prostitute

After Danny died, I didn't know what would happen, how I would cope and move on. I was back at the Children's Home where the routine of the place helped me. I knew what I would be doing every day, and the sameness of it helped my heart to heal a bit. The structure helped me go through the motions of the day, not having to make heavy decisions or deal with unstable family drama. Abby, Danny's sister, had been in the Children's Home when Danny passed away. They allowed her to go home for a couple of weeks to be with her family. Once she got back, we were in the same dorm and were allowed to bunk together. She was on the bottom bunk and I was on the top. We were both so sad and being able to talk about things helped us through Thanksgiving and Christmas, which passed by quickly.

One day she and I were sitting around with several other girls from the home, lamenting how we did not want to be there. When you're made to be someplace, even if it's not a bad place, and for me probably the best place I could have been at the time, you just want out. We had the idea—like so many times before for me—to run away. It was a quick decision that night, no preplanning and very spur-of-the-moment. We told a few other girls, and they helped us devise a plan. We knew that once we were in bed our house parent usually took a shower. We also knew there was a security guard with a flashlight who would go through all the dorms, so we needed to make our escape at a certain time. We knew the only way to get away would be to wait for our house mom to get in the shower; that way when the alarm went off she would have to get out of the shower, put something on, and then come out of her room.

Someone was posted on lookout. When the house mom got in the shower and turned it on, we waited a few minutes to make sure she was in the shower. We bolted out the fire escape as the alarm bells started shrieking in the background, scurried down the outside fire escape stairs, and sprinted across a snow-covered field into a trailer park nearby. My Aunt Judy and her three girls lived there, and we ran breathlessly—our small bags of personal items trailing behind us—to her trailer, where she took us in.

Within a few minutes of getting there, I remember hearing sirens from police cars go by. We assumed they were probably for us. Abby called one of her brothers, and he came and picked us up. He took us to his trailer out in the country, where I immediately started smoking to get high, the acrid herb filling my lungs like I was taking my first breath. We spent that night with him, and the next day he took us into Muncie. We were riding around, happy to be out of the Children's Home and getting high. We were stopped at a stoplight, and to our surprise the bus from the Children's Home that took us to school was stopped right in front of us. Abby noticed them first, and we ducked down in our seats, holding our breath, hoping they didn't see us. We couldn't believe they hadn't seen us!

Around Christmas time, I became lonely—lonely for company, for the touch of someone who cared. I wasn't the kind of girl to wait, and I began to date Jesse. Yes, the same Jesse who took me to the fair, the same Jesse who came to my dad's house with Danny for me to run away with him. I knew that my going out with Jesse would get people talking, so I fabricated a sad lie. I told people that Danny had said if he died, he would be okay with me and Jesse dating. Wow, I did this to soften the blow of my moving on so quickly. I was young and immature. I just didn't want his family mad at me. Things were never the same with his family, and I understand that now.

I called Jesse, and he picked Abby and me up that day and took us to a small, clean upstairs apartment in downtown Muncie as a place to stay because we were once more on the run. It turned out that the lady who lived in this apartment was a prostitute. I had gone to elementary school with her son, who was being raised by his grandparents. Jesse introduced us to her, and I guessed her to be in her thirties, a small lady with blonde hair. She was very nice to us and told us all sorts of stories about the johns she entertained. She filled the hours with tales of her many escapades, and she allowed us to stay with her. So, we chose to live with her, a prostitute named Candy. I know what you all are thinking: How did Jesse know her? I don't know the answer to that, and I don't really want to know the answer to that!

So, I was with Jesse: having sex, doing drugs, and trying to forget everything that had happened in the last several months. Ingrained in me was the desire to fulfill my own pleasures, brought on from years of abuse and being forced to encounter a world that small children should never have to experience. But I was no longer small; I was fifteen years old and had lived a thousand lifetimes, it seemed.

One day Jesse had left a twenty-dollar bill on the coffee table for Abby and me to buy pizza, but hours later we were still in the same spot watching TV. *Boom! Boom!* There was a loud knocking at the back door, and it flew open with a bang. A tall black man burst through the door, went right past us over to Candy, and yelled, "Gimme my money, GIMME MY MONEY!" He slapped her, cursed at her, hit her over and over as she sat there with her arms crossed over her face. We sat frozen, not knowing what to do. I instinctively knew he must be her pimp. When he turned back toward us, he saw the twenty-dollar bill still lying there and snatched it up.

I jumped off the couch and stood up resolutely. "Hey! That's MY money!" I yelled bravely.

He towered over me and in a low, defiant voice said, "It's my money now!" Then he pushed me with full force back onto the couch and stormed out the door. We sat in stunned silence while Candy touched her face to see if there was blood. I realized I had just done a very stupid thing. He had been slapping her around and I jumped right up and got in his face over twenty dollars. After rehashing the event, I felt I had escaped a potentially very dangerous situation.

Not long after this incident, Jesse told his dad and grandma that Abby and I had been on the run for a few weeks and were staying with a prostitute. They came over and told us they were turning us in. We grabbed our things and left with them, very upset because we didn't want to go back, and without having a chance to say goodbye to Candy. Regardless of her choices, good or bad, Candy was still a human being with compassion, and she took me in when I needed it. She persisted, turning tricks and I assume taking beatings from her pimp, all for the sake of getting by. I was grateful for her kindness. I will never forget her.

Jesse's dad took me to see my mom briefly before he took us back to juvie. I admitted to her what was happening, what I had done. She said she had been worried sick about me. I now know why, but at the time I didn't know she had been a prostitute or that she had been taken and used as a sex slave. I am sure all those horrible memories in her mind painted unthinkable scenarios of what might be happening to me and Abby. I hugged her and left, feeling terrible for putting my mom through two weeks of not knowing.

Reform School- an institution to which youthful offenders are sent as an alternative to prison.

When we went to court, Abby was sent back to the Children's Home. But me? I had been in and out of juvie, as well as the Children's Home. They wanted me placed out of the county, so I was being sent to White's Institute in Wabash, Indiana, now known as White's Residential & Family Services.

White's is a "nonprofit social services organization that works to redirect, rebuild and restore children, teens and families through emotional healing, personal development and spiritual growth." They had some hope for me, I believe. I had no idea how much being placed at White's would change the rest of my life.

CHAPTER 9

White's

The day I was to be picked up to go to White's couldn't come soon enough. I had been left in juvie for weeks, waiting for the day I was to be moved. I was given my street clothes in exchange for the blue uniforms I had been forced to wear. I wasted no time in shedding the uniform for a more desirable outfit, carefully did my hair, and applied makeup, relishing the small freedoms that had been denied me. These very small exceptions and pleasures, taken for granted by most, stick out to me profoundly as I look back over the years. I sat in the intake area of juvie, waiting for my probation officer to come and pick me up.

One of the main people who worked in this area was sitting at his desk, and he seemed in a particularly bad mood. He was normally a good guy, playing music for us and keeping things lively. I looked up and saw him accidentally spill his milk carton on the floor in front of his desk. When he saw that I was looking at him it seemed to infuriate him, and he walked over in front of me and dumped the rest of the milk carton at my feet. He looked me square in the eye and ordered me to clean it up. I didn't question and got the mop, soaking up the white mess as he sat there glaring at me. When my probation officer arrived to pick me up, I told her what had happened on the way. Later I learned he didn't work there anymore, though whether this incident had anything to do with it I'll never know.

White's was like a small, glistening college campus, neatly laid out on its acreage, with different divisions for the guys and girls on opposite ends and a small chapel that sat serenely to the side. There was a girl's gym and a guy's gym, a cafeteria, a diner for visits with our families, an indoor swimming pool, and cute little houses that the staff lived in. I was assigned to cottage eleven, and my house parents were Mr. and Mrs. Smith. They had just started working on campus, and I was their very first intake. This wasn't my first go-round at places like this, so I wasn't your normal fifteen-year-old. They couldn't believe that a sweet girl like me had been sent to White's. I could play the part of a sweet little girl, but they didn't know me yet, so we got along very well at first.

So many of us there were searching desperately for the love and attention we never got at home and acting out in desperate ways in our quest for it. I was a fighter and a runaway, and it took some time for them to really see this. I loved Mr. Smith, as I was sorely lacking in a father's love, but Mrs. Smith I didn't love. She reminded me too much of my stepmom, and I could never get past this. White's was a sweet escape for me with all I had gone through over the last seven months. It offered me the structure I didn't realize I needed, and I loved the campus because it wasn't like juvie or the Children's Home.

About fifteen girls lived in my division, all with problems that needed solving. Girls living together can go famously well or quickly bad. We all had our own bedroom, and that was a plus. The dress code required that you have your shirt tucked in and wear a belt. The many amenities included a restaurant that I worked at where they served burgers and shakes. I loved this place, and it gave me job skills as I learned to handle money and serve food. Every day we would have duty in the morning, with different chores to perform before we could go to the kitchen for breakfast. After breakfast there was chapel, every day but Saturday, and we would file in with the girls sitting on the right and the guys sitting on the left. After chapel we went to school. The school was a very long building, and when we entered, we weren't allowed to talk to the opposite sex, which was very strange to me. Regardless, we found a way to communicate by passing notes, sending love-struck and urgent messages back and forth. The cafeteria was the same, with the girls having one line and the guys in their own line. We filed through, picking up our food and sitting at the table designated for our division.

I hadn't been at White's long when I received a letter from my friend Shelly, the girl I met at Lakeside Middle School when I was living with my dad. She told me that her father passed away unexpectedly in a car accident and that she and her mother would like to come and visit me. I never answered her because I didn't know what to say about the loss of her father, and I believed she was better off without me. She was a good girl with a lot going for her, and I wasn't. I always regretted that. Eventually I lost the letter and her address.

White's had wonderful programs for all kinds of sports, and I ended up playing volleyball and softball. Softball was especially my favorite, and when I arrived in March it was time for the season to begin. I had played first base for the team at the Children's Home, and I stepped right in playing first base for White's. When you were sent to White's you knew you would be there for at least one year if not longer. Knowing that, I was finally able to lay aside my adult lifestyle and simply enjoy being a teenager. It gave me the opportunity to stop thinking about home life and friends and to concentrate on here and now. My life had been one long series of unpredictable and unstable events, and I had never really been able to settle in. At the Children's Home, you could be there for just a few weeks or months, never allowing you to let go and concentrate on you; I always concentrated on when I was getting out. I was finally at a place where there was peace and structure, and I felt like I could settle in and relax.

White's offered so many incredible opportunities, and one of them was a class to become a lifeguard. I was always a very good swimmer, so I took the class. It was much harder than I expected, but I passed and became a lifeguard. I was also on the varsity volleyball team. At the end of the volleyball season I won a trophy for best server. I accomplished things at White's that I never would have done at my school back home.

They tried very hard to keep boys and girls separated, but they knew it was inevitable, so they had something they called mixing. If two people liked each other and wanted to get to know one another, the guy had to write a letter to the girl to ask if she wanted to "mix" on Sunday, and it had to be approved. Mixing happened once a week and occurred during the Sunday meal. At that given time, for one hour, you could sit across the table from your crush, hold hands, and talk. When I first came to White's, I did this with several boys and dated one for a bit longer than the others. My need to have a boyfriend from the time I was in elementary school was so great.

Fair Game

Moments arrive in your life that hold bigger sway than others, and when you look back you can see that good things sometimes happen when you're not looking for them or least expect them. You realize that someone is looking out for you, even though you hadn't noticed it yet, or could not even bring yourself to believe it. Time had passed since I arrived at White's, and it was now October 1985. I had joined the choir and loved being a part of it. It was a traveling choir that went around to different churches and performed. We held a lot of practices, and it was fun mingling and singing with the other kids who were part of it as well.

One day we were practicing in the chapel and the choir director called for a break. I sat down on the steps leading up to the pulpit. All of a sudden, a boy in Levi jeans walked right in front of me, and it was all I could do to contain my fast-beating heart. I watched him as he walked by me. He was so cute I could feel my face flush with the attraction I felt. I ran into the girl's restroom with several friends and said to them, "Who is that guy? The tall dark-haired guy with the beautiful brown eyes?"

One of my girlfriends said, "Whoa, hold on. If his name is Billy, he's mine." I could feel my gut drop, and a light-headed feeling of disappointment came over me.

"So you're dating him?" I said.

"No, I'm not dating him, but I would like to," she replied. All I could think was *Heck no, if you're not dating him, he is fair game!* I was Jodie, the girl who never let anything stop her. I had a friend go up to him and tell him that I liked him. Once I saw that he liked me in return, I walked right up to him. He looked at me and smiled the most beautiful smile, and right then I asked him what his name was. He told me his name was Billy Ballenger. I asked if he was seeing anyone, and his answer was no. I asked him what level he was on, and he told me four. Me being me, I asked him if he wanted to go to Four Night with me, which was a Friday night once a month where you could hang out at the diner on campus with other students if you were on the highest level, which was four. (Four Night meant you had been there for a while, mastered doing your chores, and did not get into trouble.) He accepted my offer, and my stomach and heart did synchronized flip-flops. I was so excited I could hardly contain myself. How did I not notice this guy before? He was beyond gorgeous!

Friday couldn't come fast enough, and all week I constantly thought about every detail. White's had allowed me to be a teenager again, at least for a time, and finding someone who makes your heart flutter went along with that. Prior to meeting Billy, I had been consoling Antonio, a guy friend, over his recent breakup. I had been talking to him to help him get through it. He was devastated, so I consoled him and told him he could get over this heartbreak and move on. Friday finally came, and I excitedly made my way to the diner to meet up with Billy. I had almost arrived when Antonio ran up to me. He was so excited to surprise me and let me know that he just got promoted to four. I could tell he thought this was going to be our date night. When I was consoling him and telling him to move on, I did not mean with me!

I'm sure he could see the shock on my face. I had about fifteen feet to decide how I was going to handle this, as I knew Billy would be waiting for me inside. I knew that if I told him Billy Ballenger was waiting for me inside, he would blow up and want to fight Billy, so for the purpose of keeping Billy's gorgeous face preserved and not battered and bruised, I said nothing and walked into the diner with Antonio right beside me. Billy was with one of his friends at the counter, and he looked up at me as I walked to another table with this guy. I didn't know what to do. All I knew was that I didn't want a fight to break out, but to Billy it looked as if I had just come in with another guy and stood him up.

I felt terrible. Instead of my awesome night with Billy that I had anticipated all week long, I listened to this guy go on and on about his breakup. I could tell he liked me and wanted me to be his girlfriend. I should have been completely honest with him and told him I was just trying to help him through his breakup. Unable to convey my emotions and how I truly felt with either of the guys, he left thinking we were on the verge of a new relationship and Billy left thinking I intentionally stood him up. Both were dead wrong.

Billy left the diner that night and didn't talk to me for several days after that. I knew things had started off badly, and I so wanted to make them right. I had so many mixed feelings for him, and I didn't know how to handle them. Knowing that this other guy liked me, I tried to cool things off with him and let him know I really was not interested. At White's, everyone had a job to perform, and mine was working in the cafeteria serving food, and in the canteen or diner. Billy's was in maintenance. I wanted him to understand why I stood him up on Four Night, so when he came through the cafeteria line every day, I would try to get his attention and apologize. He was very good at ignoring me and gave me the cold shoulder. Several weeks later we had a scheduled choir trip, and I knew I couldn't tolerate Billy not knowing what had happened. My personality has never been one to hold back, so I went right up to him on the choir bus and plopped down beside him. In detail, I explained the misunderstanding then apologized. Right there on that bus Billy accepted my explanation as well as apology, and on November 3, 1985, we began dating.

I was so happy it was straightened out. I really liked Billy, and I couldn't let him go. Our beginning wasn't as easy as I thought it would be. Antonio found out that Billy and I had started going together. He went after Billy in an all-out brawl in their gym class. It wasn't a pretty sight, but Billy was prepared, and Antonio finally stopped bothering us both.

Billy and I spent every Sunday evening after that mixing, from five to six. It was the best sixty minutes of the week and the only "allowed" time to spend time together. We grew close by talking, sharing what seemed to be hundreds of notes, and spending time at choir practice. I fell hard for him. I had been with several different boys in my young life but being with Billy felt noticeably different.

One day I saw him working (maintenance) close to the boy's locker room while I was on my way to the girl's locker room to change for gym class. I snuck up to him, and we started kissing, breathlessly claiming each other as I then tore away. Billy later bragged to his friend about it, and his supervisor heard him—getting us both in trouble. It was worth it, though, because the kiss was spectacular. He was written up for it and given the option of missing his home visit or taking three swats with a paddle. He took the swats and got the home visit. I would whistle at him while I was working the cafeteria line. His house parents heard the whistle, but he covered for me so I wouldn't get in trouble and took the blame, getting himself into trouble.

The chaplains at White's at the time were Mr. and Mrs. Spencer, and Mrs. Spencer had a girls' Bible study group that I joined. I enjoyed this time with her. She also took special time with me and taught me how to do needlepoint. I really thought a lot of her for making one-on-one time with me and was grateful for it. I became a part of another girls' Bible study with Mrs. Rose, another staff member at White's. She was recently married, and we would go to her apartment on campus to hang out and talk.

One day she was telling us about a guy she went to school with and how he was a man of integrity who would not lie or deceive anyone. She told us that he would call himself out if he said something that wasn't true and apologize for it. This amazed me because I thought everyone lied. That's all I had ever really known in life was people telling lies or deceiving others; I didn't know anything about integrity and not deceiving people. This simple yet powerful story is one I have thought of often throughout my life, and its impact has echoed in my life down through the years.

Whenever I went for my home visits, I would go back to what I knew: getting high. A few weeks before I was scheduled to go home, Mr. and Mrs. Rose took me to a church in Muncie. They wanted to connect me with a church in my hometown so I would continue going to church once I was out. I thought this was a good idea. I did not know anyone in my hometown who went to church, so I was excited to meet new people my age that went. It was a beautiful church. We went to the youth group service that morning, and I was nervous but filled with excitement. When we walked into the youth group and were introduced to everyone, I had a big smile on my face and told everyone my name. I expected them to accept me with open arms, but that isn't what happened. No one wanted to talk to me or even looked half interested in getting to know me. I left there that day knowing I would not be returning. I so badly wanted to become a part of something good and to meet new friends, but instead I left defeated and hurt. One more brick laid in the wall of my identity that said DEFEAT, REJECT, UNWORTHY, UNWANTED.

Time's Up

As the days faded one into another, I soon found that my time at White's was up and I would be let out. I had arrived at White's in March 1985, and it was now fourteen months later, May 1986. I was sixteen years old. My mom and great grandma picked me up. As we left, we saw Billy walking to the boys' gym and pulled over to say a quick goodbye. I was happy he got to meet my mom and grandma, and we each said that we loved each other and snuck a quick kiss. We didn't know when Billy would get out, but we were hoping soon.

White's was now in my rearview mirror. Being at White's gave me opportunities I likely wouldn't have had otherwise, and to this day I am thankful. It gave me true confidence, built up my self-esteem, and removed some of those bricks of my identity that were cemented in lies. I needed a time-out from my regular life, and White's was the perfect place to do so. The structure and stability helped me to set some of my priorities in the right direction. Billy would tell you he felt the same way.

I was a little sad to say goodbye, especially since Billy was still there. I was happy that we declared to one another that we would stay together, but to be perfectly honest, I thought that once I left, he would start dating someone else at White's. Even though I wanted it to work out, I truthfully didn't expect it to. We did not live by each other outside of White's. We lived a couple of hours away from each other. You know how most girls have a fairy-tale view of life, expecting to meet prince charming, get married, and live happily ever after? I don't ever remember a time that I did. My expectation was to meet and marry a man, have a marriage that lasted a few years, then get divorced. I never had high hopes for much, and I accepted that relationships just don't last, no matter how much you want them to.

BILLY AND A FRIEND

JODIE BALLENGER

MY GREAT GRANDMA GOLDIE VISITING ME AT WHITE'S

ME AND MY COUNSELOR FROM WHITE'S

CHAPTER 11

Billy's on the Run

I arrived back at Middletown Gardens, happy to be out of White's but incredibly heartbroken that Billy was still there. I gave up hope that it could ever work between us. We didn't have a phone, and the only one available for use was a payphone down the street. All these thoughts descended upon me of how far apart we were, with no cars to travel back and forth to see each other, and no means of communication. After my release, I was put on probation – as I'd been since sixth grade along with mandatory summer school and checking in with my probation officer. Seeing Billy seemed a huge improbability. Engrained patterns operate like deep ruts in a driveway, and your vehicle is incapable of breaking free from the crevices that hold your tires. The vehicle of my mind was stuck in those ruts so deep it didn't look like I could ever drive out of them. I knew being with Billy would never work out. So, I began seeing other guys, my body and feelings for him betraying what I felt. I let familiar impulses overtake me and started partying a lot and sleeping around.

One day I came home from summer school and there he was—Billy. He had served his time, gotten out, and had his Aunt Brenda drive him up to see me. I was stunned, all manner of thought processes thrown out the window. He had come to see me first...me. What was this new and odd feeling that rushed through me? Were there people who remained true even when old ways crept in? I wanted to believe that and was so shocked that he hadn't forgotten about me. His lifestyle and the way he had grown up were in complete opposition to the way I had grown up. His thoughts were not my own. We were both still so young, but could he teach me how to truly love? How to be faithful and trust again?

I took his hand, and we went to my room. He told me, "Jodie, I missed you. We are going to make it. We are going to stay together." I knew he had guessed there had already been other guys. He knew me so well and yet pursued me as a prize, and I gave myself completely to him. We had sex in my room for the first time that day, my mom and his aunt just steps away in the kitchen. I wanted him to know that I cared for him so deeply, even with my many failings and deep flaws. It was a flimsy offering, as there is so much more to relationships than just sex, but it was what I had known, seen, and all I knew to give. Billy had to leave to go home with his aunt that day, but he said he would be back.

Billy was raised by his Aunt Mary and Uncle Danny, who had watched him a lot since his birth but legally adopted him when he was three years old. His biological mom and dad both were alcoholics and addicted to drugs, so they gave Billy to his mom's sister to raise. He grew up with a cousin/sister that was six or seven years older than him. Both his adopted mom and biological mom came from a large family of ten children. When he was ten years old his mom Mary, told Danny she wanted a divorce. She had been having an affair at work with the security guard. Billy said that is when everything changed for him. His mom moved to a trailer with the security guard, who also left his spouse. Billy said that it was hard on Danny, but eventually Danny remarried as well.

This is where the difficulty and struggle with stepparents come in. Billy had a hard time adjusting to life with stepparents. His stepdad, the once security guard now truck driver, was hard to live with. His mom worked the graveyard shift as a CNA at a local nursing home. So, when he was living with them, he was alone most of the time. They lived in the country with no other kids to play with, so Billy was terribly lonely. He had to be quiet during the day so his mom could sleep. He wasn't allowed to watch TV or listen to music. If they ever had company he was told to go outside and play, so even when he thought he was finally going to be able to talk to people, and be around them, he was forbidden. Anyone who knows Billy knows that he thrives being around people. Isolation was the worst kind of torture you could subject Billy to. He was not really getting the love and affection a child needs.

When Billy was thirteen, his father, Danny, had gotten divorced and remarried for the third time to a woman he met at a factory he worked at. She had three boys, and when he lived with them it was even worse than living with his adopted mother, Mary. Billy struggled with this as well, a teenage boy living in a small trailer with a new stepmom and three step-brothers. At times the tension was so thick that he and his stepmom did not speak for months. He would try to communicate with her, and she would just pretend he was invisible and refuse to respond in any way. With matters escalating at his dad's, Billy ran away to his mom's. That did not last long either, as Billy found living in the country in lonely isolation with virtually no freedoms too much to bear. He ran away again to his grandparents', where he remained until being sent to White's by the court system. He said that he loved it at his grandparents' house, and his grandfather gave him purpose. He felt safe and loved there. When it came time to be taken to White's, Billy's adoptive parents both drove him there. On the way Mary told him, "Billy, you never know. You might meet your future wife here!"

Billy had a strained relationship with both sets of parents and did not want to live with either one when he got out of White's. So he stayed with one of his aunts and uncles. He started working for his uncle painting barn roofs. Shortly after he got out, his uncle dropped him off to paint a barn roof. He slipped off the roof and twisted his ankle, which sent him over the edge. He decided right then that he was determined to come see me. He found the strength and walked several miles to another aunt's house and asked her to bring him to my house. After our visit that day, his aunt dropped him off at his aunt and uncle's house where he was staying. They knew he had left town and informed him that he was to see his probation officer that next morning. His uncle woke him up at 7:30 that morning and told him to be ready by 8:30 to go see his PO. Billy jumped out of bed frantically, got dressed in a rush, and ran away to be with me, with just the clothes on his back. Keep in mind this was before cell phones. It took him three hours and five rides hitchhiking to get to me.

After he arrived at my house, my mom sent him back to my room. He knocked on the door, and when I opened it I could not believe he was back so soon. He told me he had run away. I was initially mad at him because I wanted him to keep out of trouble and live a good life, but I was selfishly happy that he was there with me.

We were so young, and we stayed at my place for a bit. My mom and Austin went through yet another of their seemingly endless spats. Austin had just received a check from his Native reservation for four thousand dollars, so he got himself a room at the Holiday Inn for the weekend. The next day, he and my mom made up, so Billy and I stayed the next two days and nights in the room. It was like a mini honeymoon without the wedding or the marriage certificate. We even ordered room service for every meal, which was quite the surprise for Austin when he came back to check out of the room and found he owed more money for all the food we ordered.

Upon returning home, my mom wouldn't let Billy stay there for long. My sister had an apartment that she rarely stayed at, so Billy and I moved in. Austin would pick me up every day for summer school then drop me back off at the apartment. One day, on the way to Central High School, we noticed we had three police officers surrounding us—one in front, one beside, and one behind. I knew something was up, and my heart pounded as I realized that once more the law was closing in. When I got to the school that day, I had to meet with my PO. She asked me about Billy and said that he was on the run. She told me that if they found him with me, I would be sent to the girl's school. I was overwhelmed by feelings of panic because I could not be locked up again. I loved Billy with all my heart and once more experienced the sensation of feeling trapped with no way out.

Time to Go

My mom and Austin showed up with bags of McDonald's food later that evening at the apartment and told us that Billy had to go back. They liked Billy and seemed disturbed themselves about his having to leave. Momentous occasions throughout my young life were often marked by the bringing of food, things I couldn't afford to eat on a regular basis, as a way of comforting me against bad news. A clearly marked bag of cheeseburgers meant imminent change. The next day, after Billy had been on the run for two weeks, we dropped him off in Franklin, Indiana, near the jail, where he reluctantly turned himself in. He lied and told them he had not been with me, and I'm sure they had a hard time believing him. But he was trying to protect me. The Monday after Billy turned himself in, his adopted mom, Mary, came to visit him. He told her he would be willing to live with her again if she would allow him to come see me on a regular basis. The only stipulations she had was that he would have to get a job and pay for his own travel to come see me and that he had to sleep on the couch, not in my bed, while visiting.

He agreed to go back to his mom's house. He got a job working with his Uncle Danny painting cars, and that next weekend he began taking bus trips to my house. He would be dropped off at the K-mart in Greenwood, Indiana, and take a city bus to the main bus depot in downtown Indianapolis. He would then catch an ABC Coach line to Muncie. What should have been an hour--and-a-half drive could take three to four hours. So that summer every weekend Billy would get on a bus and come see me. This was such an exciting time for us. We desperately wanted to be together, and we had decided that nothing would keep us apart.

School began in the fall with Billy in eleventh grade in Franklin, and myself starting my tenth-grade year at Muncie South. Billy wasn't working his job anymore during school and ran out of money to come and see me. This was a tragedy for us. He decided it was time to run away once again, and he and a friend hitched a ride via several different people, the last one being a truckload of drunken boys. They were so drunk Billy took over driving a stick shift for the first time in his life. The severity of the events occurring—running away, promiscuity, immaturity, inability to have a truly adult relationship, and dysfunctional choices—didn't seem to sink into our skulls. We only knew we wanted to be together and would find a way to do that no matter what the cost—and trust me, it did cost us.

My mom, again, wouldn't let Billy stay at our house, so a friend delivered Billy and his friend to an abandoned house in Muncie. I was upset with Mom for not allowing Billy to stay with us. It seemed my whole life she never truly parented me in a healthy way, and when it counted most— or at least when I thought it counted—she decided to be a mom. My teenage mind couldn't set it down. Billy and his friend stayed at the abandoned house for one night, after which the friend he ran away with wanted to return home to pick up a check. So he and Billy hitchhiked back to Franklin. His friend decided he'd had enough of being on the run and went back home. Billy got in contact with his biological mother, who put him up for a night, and the next day she dropped him off at my ex-boyfriend Danny's (who had died in the car accident) mom's, and she allowed him to stay. It wasn't the same house that Danny had lived in before he died, as the despair over what had happened caused his family to move. His mom and dad were now divorced.

Billy was floating in between various places, on the run from the authorities as he was still underage until February. We dyed his hair, going from his natural dark brown to blond. It turned out bright orange, the color going wrong in the worst way. My mom was extremely inconsistent about allowing Billy to stay at our house. There were times she would, and then other times she would go into a rage and kick him out. She didn't know that at night he would knock on the window of my room and crawl into bed with me. She was extremely unpredictable with what she allowed and didn't, and finally I simply didn't care what she said because there was no winning with her, no matter what I did or didn't do. I decided to do what made me happy and being with Billy is what made me happy.

One day while watching TV, we saw shadows passing by the windows, creeping around the property. A chill ran down my spine as Billy ran into my sister's room where her boyfriend, Don, was.

"The cops are here! I need to hide under the bed!" he said. Billy crawled quickly underneath, and the boyfriend, in a panic, rushed to hide as well. He pulled a blanket over himself on the floor, attempting to appear like a pile of dirty clothes. My sister opened the front door as casually as she could, and the cops stood there staunchly. To our utter surprise, they told us they were looking for her boyfriend and not Billy. As they walked around inside our house searching, I wondered nervously where he had hidden. When they entered the bedroom, I saw the blanket over someone and thought with dread they were going to lift that blanket and find Billy, and he would have to explain why he was hiding. A rush of relief went through me as they lifted the blanket and it was Don and not

Billy. When the cops left, Billy crawled out from under the bed with a deep sigh, releasing the tense fear that had been lodged in his throat. I couldn't believe he hadn't been caught!

Another time, Billy and I were sitting on my bed when we heard a loud banging on the front door. We looked out and could see it was the sheriff. Billy rolled off the bed and underneath it, and I went to open the door. They showed me a picture of Billy, saying, "We're looking for this boy, Billy. Is he here?" I wasn't shy around the police because they'd been in my life for a very long time, and I was belligerent if anything. But this time I played it cool and slipped on my pitiful face. I let tears stream down and said, "You mean he's gone? I can't believe he ran away again!" I was a good faker, and we avoided Billy getting caught for months and months.

There was also a time when Austin and Billy were in my room putting together a stereo system while I was at summer school. The police came and started talking to Austin, and Billy was standing right next to him with his very orange hair and dark brown eyebrows. The police showed Austin a picture of Billy and asked if he had seen him. Billy contorted his face, and they both said they had not seen him, and the police left.

The tales and trials of Billy's time on the run ended when he turned eighteen the next February, and just like that they stopped looking for him because he became an adult. I had turned seventeen in December, and we were convinced that we wanted to be together forever, but my mom wasn't happy that I was with him. As usual, she bounced back and forth between liking Billy and helping me be with him, and then ripping it out from underneath me. Looking back, I realize she was panicking because she had no control at this point and knew she was losing me for good. She could no longer jerk me back and forth between her maddening double binds and unpredictable, ever-changing rules.

Finally . . . We Make the Rules

We decided to rent my sister Adrian's old apartment and be on our own, which we loved. Having our own place, our own things, and no one to tell us what to do was a welcome respite from the chaos and drama of both our families. It didn't matter that we were still very young and incredibly immature. We determined that we would make it somehow. We moved into the two bedroom apartment on Walnut and Ninth Street sometime in early May.

After Billy turned eighteen, he got a job at Marsh's grocery store down the road. There never seemed to be enough food in our home. Food. When I think of it, I see in my mind's eye empty cupboards and empty refrigerators throughout my life, with hungry bellies never quite filled, and a mom who noticed but felt there was nothing she could really do about it. Billy's first check went to buy groceries to fill that void.

Endearing moments can occur despite oppressed lives full of confusion and fear, and when Billy asked me to marry him early that year as we lay embracing one day, I excitedly accepted his proposal. I could see that he was good at heart, that he wanted me for who I was, and that he would try to give us the best life possible even though we didn't have much. We picked out the date of July 18, 1987, for our wedding and started planning the details. I loved Billy deeply, to the degree I could, through my dysfunction, my pain, and the twisted lens through which I viewed life as the result of my upbringing. Both of us were extremely immature, and our gauge of measuring right from wrong was corrupted and warped. Billy had more of a grasp of these principles but had succumbed to the addictive drama and wild antics of the crew that surrounded my family's life.

Although we had slept together many times, it was still a surprise to us when just a few weeks after Billy's proposal we found out I was pregnant. My dad still had full custody of me during this time, and he agreed to sign the papers for me to be able to get married. I also was released from probation around this time. Living with Billy was like slipping into a soft pair of pajamas; it was comfortable and felt right to me. Compared to my prior environments, the sometimes volatile and unsettling events that happened in my life with Billy, seemed minor. But we were products of the distortion of our childhoods, and that still meant turbulence to come. There were times we fought like men, and I don't say that lightly. I had learned to be a scrapper, a fighter, and could hold my own with anyone. It wasn't uncommon for us to come to blows physically in those early years.

A week or so before the wedding was set to occur, Billy and I got into a terrible fight. In the heat of the argument I flew out the door and took off down the street. I was raging down the street, pregnant and fuming, when from behind me I heard Billy running after me. He proceeded to pick me up and carry me home. Let it be known that I allowed him to pick me up and carry me home, because no one did anything to me that I didn't want them to at this point in my life. Never again. The pregnancy, though a surprise, caused me to move toward the future with a more determined and hopeful outlook. Now there was someone other than myself to care for, to get ready for. So, we looked forward to our approaching wedding. I wanted to do what was right for this baby. I wanted to be a better parent than mine were to me.

CHAPTER 12

Going to the Chapel

My life had been hell-bent on dragging me down with it, and I did a pretty good job of going along with its every whim. But I did want more; I wanted a better life and was clawing my way toward finding it. Even when my volatile nature wanted to take over, I fought it. I had partied from the time I was nine years old, and I was ready to lay it all down. I was finishing my tenth-grade year, and the wedding was fast approaching. Even though we were doing better than we had before, we still didn't have much. We put our heads together, Billy and I, to make the wedding happen.

My Uncle Sonny, my maternal grandma's brother, owned Miller's Flower Shop, one that had been in business for many years in Muncie. He was also a pastor, and without him our wedding wouldn't have taken place. I wanted our wedding to be special, but on a very limited budget and with no place to turn, we knew we'd have to take what was offered. He opened his church to us as we flew by the seat of our pants on love, exhilaration, and a ray of hope. He provided all the flowers, only asking one thing in return: Billy and I had to go to his church at least two times before the wedding. Many times in my life, small open windows appeared where a dim ray of light shone through to me. This was one of those rays that one day I would look back on and realize someone was looking out for Billy and me and showing us hope for change, for peace, and for a future.

Despite my anger toward my dad for abandoning me when I needed him most, I decided to ask him for $180 to rent my wedding dress and Billy's tux. This was a very difficult decision for me because I had vowed never to ask him for anything after he refused to provide for me as a young child. It still stung knowing that he always had money but chose to leave me in poverty. I held him at arm's length, not wanting to ask him for more than I had to. I craved for him to love me the way a daddy should love his daughter, yet my anger and pride wanted nothing from him. I had Tonia, a school friend, and Danny's sister Abby as my bridesmaids. My only rule was that they wear dresses with pink in them—they planned to dress up in their swirly prom dresses. Along with my eleven-year-old niece Karen, my sister Kelli's daughter, and Billy's two best men and his nephew Tommy, we were quite the sight, young kids pretending to be adults.

Dropping the Bomb

The night before the wedding found me a bit anxious, all the stress of the last-minute plans for the ceremony pressing in on me. I knew it was what I wanted more than anything, and as the baby kicked inside of me, I calmed myself. But my life was full of crazy ups and downs, like riding on a rollercoaster, the car leaving the track and careening out of control to the ground with a deafening crash. My mother came over that evening, nervously fidgeting. I was immediately suspicious because she didn't act like a cat on a hot tin roof often. She said she had something to tell me.

"What is it, Mom?" I asked, not yet alarmed at the tone of her voice, even though I should have been.

"Jodie, there's something I've been wanting to tell you for a while," she faltered, her voice cracking just a bit. I cocked my head and looked at her expectantly, not sure I wanted anything else rocking the boat at this moment in my life. I always knew her to be straightforward and in-your-face.

"What is it?" I repeated.

"Your dad, well, he isn't really your dad," she sputtered, the words falling like endless rain inside me. My dad wasn't my dad? WHAT?! Why was it necessary to tell me this now? "Your real dad is your uncle," she disclosed bluntly.

I was taken aback and sat down to steady myself. "What do you mean my dad is my uncle?" My voice came out shrill.

She shook her head, that old craziness inside of her stirring up to a crescendo. "What I mean is your birth dad is your Aunt Lisa's husband, your Uncle John." And with that she left abruptly, leaving me with one more pot stirred up and bubbling. I grappled with this new declaration as the wild, frayed edges of information dangled in the wind.

The wedding was scheduled to start at 6:30 in the evening, and the day dawned with promise and went wild from there. I had every intention of it going just as planned, but my mom had thrown a serious monkey wrench in the works the night before with her announcement. You roll with life's punches, and this day was no different, but I felt like I'd been punched in the gut in a way that left me paralyzed. I had everything laid out, ready to go, but I was still a kid having a baby who was stepping into a marriage with everything stacked against it.

While on the way to the church, my bridesmaids and I were stopped by a train barreling down the tracks. I started to panic thinking Billy would believe I wasn't coming. I was half an hour late to my own wedding, running into a church full of waiting people in my street clothes, not having wanted to change until I arrived. I smiled a timid, apologetic smile and, along with my bridesmaids, ran to change in a flash.

I was thankful my dad was there to walk me down the aisle, where I said "I do" to Billy Ballenger. Our motley crew of friends dressed in prom dresses, rented tuxes, and one groomsman in his oily mechanic clothes made for memorable photos. It was a comical sight. We were so young, but we were married, and I was happy. A small group of family and friends turned out to celebrate with us. We were officially Mr. and Mrs. William Ballenger.

On our honeymoon night, we went back to stay at our two-bedroom apartment because there was no money for a fancy trip. We'd received a small amount of money for the wedding, around $150, and we used that to go stay with Billy's biological mom the next week. It was nice to be out from our area for a bit, even if it meant staying with family and not being alone. When we returned, we began married life and I entered the eleventh grade.

It was a strange yet proud thing to return to school as a married wife. I had a good thing going because I was in a work-study program: half a day at school and the other half working as a waitress. But during roll call, several of my teachers continued to use my maiden name, and each time they did this I corrected them. Finally, they all began to use my married name except for one teacher. He harassed me, questioned me, and continually called me by my maiden name just to annoy me. I insisted he call me by my married name, but he refused to do it. I felt greatly disrespected, especially being pregnant and already feeling vulnerable. After enduring two weeks of this treatment, and only two weeks into my junior year, I dropped out of school for good. I lost my job as a waitress because it was through the work-study program.

OUR WEDDING PHOTO WITH OUR PARENTS

JULY 18,1987

CHAPTER 13

Party Life

In the months leading up to our daughter's birth, our apartment became a place of heavy partying. Billy and his best friend, Brian, drank and smoked weed every day. Billy didn't just casually drink, he drank to get drunk. He had begun working as a pizza delivery man at Domino's Pizza near Ball State University after he quit at Marsh's grocery store, and I loved this arrangement. For me it meant pizza and Pepsi every day after he got off work. The weeks and months passed as we awaited the tiny, fragile life to come barging into our dysfunctional one, and I gained sixty-five pounds during the pregnancy. I was miserable. But life rolled on, and three weeks overdue on November 20, 1987, our daughter Arminda was finally born. She was born on a Friday at 5:49 p.m., weighed 8 lbs 7 oz, and was 21 inches long. We fell in love with her instantly. She had an adorable tumble of dark curls, dimples, and her daddy's gentle brown eyes.

Immersing an infant into utter chaos has no place to go but a downward spiral. We continued allowing the alcohol and drugs in our home, with unsavory and dangerous people, known felons, coming and going. I began to smoke pot again after I had Mindy because this was the one vice I had a hard time giving up. Marijuana was always a way of escape for me, and now a way to medicate myself from the madhouse our home was fast becoming. My partying days were over, but I didn't know how to stop this snowball that was gaining density day by day, becoming a lethal force that Billy didn't seem to want to stop.

I despised the dark cloud of oppression that was settling around us. I was there in the house with Billy and our friends, but my heart wasn't in it anymore. From a very young age I had spent my life drinking and drugging, with no moral compass except to follow the depraved ways of my family. I was done with it all and didn't want this for Mindy, but Billy was just getting started. He hadn't grown up with this lifestyle, and now he was losing himself in the seductive addiction of it. We made sure Mindy had what she needed, but during this time we were not good parents, and it felt as though the cycle my mother, father, and grandparents had established was continuing full force with us.

Billy was still delivering pizzas for Domino's, and the money was good. They were inundated with orders and deliveries, so he stayed very busy. Our landlord had sold us a sweet little car, a Horizon, and it was the best car we ever had. I like to say that we owned a string of "disposable cars" we paid fifty dollars for, and when they died, we disposed of them and got another one. We owned over fifty of these disposable cars. This Horizon, though, it was my favorite and in very good shape. I was proud to be driving it and couldn't believe we had something this nice to call our own.

One day, though, there was an accident when Billy was delivering a pizza on a main road and forgot to put the blinker on. As he was delivering the pizza, *bang!* Someone ran right into the back of the car. We didn't have any insurance, and our little car was gone along with Billy's driver's license. I was furious at him. He convinced his manager to let his friend drive while he delivered pizzas after that. It worked for a time, his friend driving him around to deliver pizzas, but it didn't work for long. They both grew weary of it and Billy soon quit, which was a financial blow as he had made decent money. We were still newly married with a small infant, and flat broke.

Billy grew more and more violent during this time as he partied, drank, and reveled in everything illegal and corrupt that came his way. He loved the reputation he had in the streets as being a good fighter who did not take crap from anyone, and someone you definitely did not want to mess with. He thought these "friends" were the family he had always been looking for during his lonely days cooped up in the country. I was along for the ride and couldn't stop it, and it was a recipe for disaster. We owed rent money and another month was coming due when we decided to pack up our things in the middle of the night and sneak out without paying the rent. We felt we had no choice.

CHAPTER 14

Ghosts

Before we move on, there are some bizarre little side stories that must be told. Ones that might give you shivers and question everything you've ever been told. Maybe you believe in spooky happenings and supernatural tales, or maybe you shake your head in disbelief. I firmly believe in the existence of spirits, ones that tickle the back of your neck while you sleep or move things around, paralyzing you with fear. I would never make these stories up. Let me tell you why.

Our first apartment was situated in an old house with a long stairway to reach the second floor. It was creaky and rickety and set an eerie tone for the small apartment. All the rooms were carpeted. This made for muffled walking, as carpet tamps down most sounds. Yet several times when Billy was coming home from work very late at night, he heard what sounded like a woman in high heels walking on hardwood floors. Click-clack, click-clack they went, walking through the rooms, goosebumps appearing on his arms as the hair stood up on the back of his neck. Along with the echoes of high heels came the tinkle of laughter that reached his ears with horror.

One morning, we got up and headed out to have breakfast, leaving the apartment like any other normal day. When we arrived back home after eating, I found my sister standing in the middle of the apartment, which was filled with smoke that hung in the air like swirling tendrils.

"What is going on?" I demanded, not understanding what was happening.

She yelled, "You left your deep fryer on! You almost burned the whole place down!"

I looked at Billy, and we shook our heads and said there was no way, as we left for breakfast as soon as we woke up. Had the deep fryer been on from last night, we would have smelled the smoke. When we left, there was no smoke. We knew something had to have turned it on. Was it the laughing lady with high heels who click-clacked her way through our apartment?

The story that makes me stop and ponder to this day and raises the hairs on the back of my neck, is the one I'll relate next. I was sitting in the living room, and Billy and Austin left to go somewhere. On top of our stereo system were the wineglasses we drank out of for our wedding toast. They stood there, side by side, neat and tall. All of a sudden, I glanced over that way, feeling an eerie sensation. Right before my unbelieving eyes, one of the glasses slowly rose into the air. I felt paralyzed and frozen to my seat. My heart stopped beating, and as if by an unseen arm, the glass moved across the room and came to a stop right in front of me. I stared at it, in mesmerized terror, and suddenly it fell to the ground. I ran down the steps and outside to our car, where Billy and Austin were getting ready to leave, and told them breathlessly what had just happened. All three of us went back to the apartment and saw the wineglass lying on the carpet, unbroken. They looked at each other, picked up the glass, and set it on top of the stereo with the other. Billy then tapped it with his finger in tiny increments to see how far it could go; it fell straight down and crashed to the floor and shattered into pieces. There was no way I was going to stay at that apartment that day. I insisted on going with them!

The day we decided to leave the apartment in the middle of the night, skipping out on rent before anyone was awake outside to catch us leaving, we heard what sounded like a large group of kids playing outside. We looked with alarm at each other because it was four o'clock in the morning in the dead of winter, and there would be no kids outside playing. We went to the window and drew back the blinds slowly, dread filling us as we peeked outside. There was no one there as the wind forlornly whipped twigs across Walnut Street. I shuddered as we took our things and moved out, leaving that apartment behind. I was glad to be gone and glanced back up as we left, chills sweeping down my spine. We were relieved to get out of there and away from the evil that seemed to be haunting it.

CHAPTER 15

The Thunder Rolls

We arrived in Fort Wayne with little to our name, just our baby, each other, and a few possessions. We stayed with my mom for a while and eventually moved into a house right next to my sister Kelli. I found a factory job, and Billy worked drywall and plaster with Kelli's father-in-law. It worked for a while, but the unbearable urge to party was so strong in Billy that he went back to Muncie nearly every weekend to an onslaught of drinking, then back to work the next Monday. We were fighting and arguing a lot, so much that I feared for what would come of our relationship.

Late one night we had a dreadful argument, and the yelling and screaming had reached a zenith that spiraled out of control. Billy didn't like that we were living away from friends, so secluded that people couldn't just stop in and hang out. He wanted out, and that very night he packed up some things and left me and our baby girl and went back to Muncie to drown himself in the party scene.

I was upset, yes, but I expected it. I didn't think it would last anyway. I was okay for a few days, and then I received a call from my mom, who told me Billy had been seen with a girl. I was devastated. I thought I was okay with him leaving until I heard he was with someone else. What the heck! The open relationships I had experienced and seen my parents' pattern, were being perpetuated in our marriage. So that weekend my mom and I went to Muncie, picked up my sister Adrian and her son, and went around town asking questions.

I had an ax handle with me that I had gotten from a guy who told me Billy was at one of his parties and was flirting with a girl. I went over to Billy's best friend Brian's house and called him out. Billy walked up to me, and I started aggressively pushing him, and my mom and sister joined in the assault against him. I told him I was going to take the car, so he tried to force me into the car, but I kept kicking the door open while he was trying to shut the door. Billy turned to realize that my sister Adrian was roaring at him in her car, her face twisted in a demented snarl. In a panic, he grabbed the door of the car and jumped in the air at the same time her car made impact with our car, exactly where he had been standing! Had he not jumped in the air and landed on the hood of her car, he would have lost his legs in the collision. Reaching down inside our car he grabbed a baseball bat and in a violent rage busted her windshield out. I sped off in his car, burning rubber as I left. The next day I went to file for divorce. I knew there was no repair for all the bad that had happened in our relationship.

A week or two later I returned to Muncie, having been summoned to the first court procedure for our divorce hearing. As I drove into town with a heavy heart, I passed a car wash and saw Billy there with a group of friends. I turned around and informed him why I was there and that the divorce was proceeding forward. Mindy was with me, and Billy desperately wanted to see her and be with her for a while. I decided that every dad needs to see his child and left her with him for several hours. I told him I'd be at Abby's house and to bring her there when he was done. Did I have ulterior motives? No, I really wanted Mindy to be able to see her dad, as she was just four months old and couldn't understand what was happening. I was so sad for her. I'm sure she noticed that her daddy hadn't been around. Later that night Billy brought her back to Abby's house. He wanted us to stay in Muncie with him, to work at being a family again. I wanted him back, and we talked many things out that night.

The next morning, we all went over to Brian's house to get his things, and we went into Brian's sister Debra's room where Billy announced in what I thought was an oddly strange interaction with her that we were getting back together. We didn't go to the divorce hearing scheduled for that day. We rented the upstairs apartment above Abby's that day and made a trip to Fort Wayne to gather our things and bring them back, settling into our new apartment to give it another try. It was a small one-bedroom apartment but was furnished, so all we really needed was our dishes and utensils, plus personal items. We were back in an area where friends could stop by and have a drink or smoke, a place where Billy felt he could have a little bit of both worlds. Neither of us was working, but we knew we would find work eventually.

Enough

Just when you feel that things are coming together, a fateful event crashes into your reality and shocks you out of your state of denial. Brian's cousin came by for a visit, and she told me that Billy had been with Debra—Brian's sister and someone I had considered a friend—while we were split up. I looked at her in shock, and then I began to put the pieces together of many memories that should have hinted at this affair. They flooded my brain like a raging waterfall. We used to party at her house and had even spent New Year's Eve there. Debra had mentioned a few little things that needed done at her home, and I sent Billy over there to help her when we lived right across the alley from her. My head felt as though it would explode with the realization that I had sent my man over to help a deceitful damsel in distress. What a hard lesson to learn.

Memories flooded my mind of her flirting with him, and I never addressed it because she did that with all the guys. I felt overwhelmed with a sense of betrayal and hurt. When Billy came home that evening, I confronted him about it, and he flat-out denied it. My heart was broken now recalling all the moments I had tried to dismiss and make excuses for, the "too-friendly" gestures I thought were just her personality or my imagination. When Billy left me and went back to Muncie—I thought to be near his friends—it was also to run into her arms and bed. Now I knew why the strange encounter happened, when he took Mindy and me into Debra's room, waking her up to announce that we were back together. He was going to go down lying about it, refusing to be honest. I'd been so naïve. I felt violated, betrayed, and just plain stupid.

During this time, Billy's biological mother and younger sister needed a place to stay, so we told them they could stay with us for a while. We almost never turned anyone in need away. However, our relationship was in no shape to handle anyone else living with us. Billy's biological mother was a woman driven by selfish motives and enslaved to addictions to alcohol, drugs, and the party life. There wasn't anyone she wouldn't use for her own benefit, even her son. We should have known this would be a recipe for disaster. She was with us for nearly a month before we kicked her out when she stole from us.

One night, deep into the wee hours, I awoke to find Billy and his biological mother gone. It wasn't long before I found out they were at Debra's and Brian's house partying. I felt sick to my stomach and my heart shattered. He had promised me he would not go around her, but he did. I was done with Billy's betrayals. Although both times Billy was with Debra were when we were separated, we were still married. Unfortunately, marriage was never a reason for staying faithful in any of my family or friends. I had grown up seeing this very thing happen to, everyone around me. I could no longer bear living a life with Billy that was full of lies and half-truths, so in broken desperation I called a women's shelter for help. They sent a police car for us and waited in the apartment while I gathered a few necessary things.

They drove us to an office downtown where they started asking me all kinds of personal questions. One question made me very uneasy. "Do you and your husband fight, Jodie?"

"Yes," I answered truthfully. "We do get physical with each other, but he has never touched our daughter." In looking back, Billy was never an abuser. Anytime we became physical, it was because I physically attacked him in the same way I often saw my mother attack the men in her life. Only then would Billy sometimes fight back for his own safety and defense. After the questioning ended, they examined Mindy and asked me to take her clothes off. They looked her over carefully, examining her entire body. After they were done, they told me why they were being so thorough. Billy's biological mother had called them, after we kicked her out of the house, and said that Billy had been "lighting matches and burning Mindy with them." They'd been checking her for burn marks.

Though I was furious at Billy for what we were going through, I told them in no uncertain terms that he loved his daughter, had never hurt her, and never would. This woman who birthed Billy but was never a mother to him dared to tell lies about her own son. Thank God the lies could easily be proved wrong by examining Mindy. She had stolen money from us and reported terrible lies. It took me years to get over this. This mighty wind of discouragement fanned the fire from the volcano of rage within me. I retreated into my numb space, that place where I felt little emotion, checking out from the raging waves of despair threatening to destroy me.

Mindy and I stayed in the women's shelter for about three weeks. I had made up my mind that if I ever saw Billy inadvertently, I would turn around and walk the other way and ignore him. The shelter helped me get assistance to obtain an apartment on our own, and I was ready for a fresh start. I had instructed our friends not to tell Billy where we lived so he wouldn't try to change my mind. I was on my way to see Abby at her house one day, and when I pulled up, I saw Billy exiting the house. My heart raced as I turned, quickly trying to get Mindy back in the car to make a fast getaway. I didn't want to see him. But persuasion is Billy's middle name, and he convinced me to take the time to talk to him. I sat there staring at him blankly, a deep red ring of hickeys circling his neck, taunting me. The hurt pulsed in me like an open wound.

"Jodie, I miss you and want to be with you and our baby," he pleaded. "Please forgive me."

I glared at him hard, pinning him with my narrowed eyes, and demanded, "Who are the hickeys from?"

"Debra," he admitted.

My heart exploded in a somersault. I then asked him all the questions I'd asked him before, the ones he had denied to my face. This time he confessed. He told me everything down to being with her after our first breakup and then this time, our second breakup. He didn't hold anything back. I was at war within myself because I didn't want to be involved in chaos anymore. I wanted normalcy, stability, and so much more. Yet that part of me that had learned at a young age to physically fight for what I wanted raised its head, and I looked straight into his eyes and said, "I will get back with you on one condition: that you take me over to Debra's right now and knock on her door and get her outside so I can beat her up. I won't do it any other way."

He nodded his head and agreed. Looking back at this now, it was a junior high move. We were both so immature and had been programmed to deal with issues in the most dysfunctional ways.

What was my reasoning? I had seen this scenario play out a million times in my life by everyone around me. Guy cheats on girl and leaves her for another girl, gets mad at that girl and goes back to the first girl, and this cycle keeps going around and around and around for their whole lives—one big ring of mistrust, betrayal, and misery. I had reasoned in my head that if I went over and beat up the girl who had been with my man, and we separated again and he went back to her, she would surely turn him away, and if not they could just have each other!

I was a fighter, but with everything that had happened I was at a low point in my life and I turned to liquid courage. I began to drink – heavily. I felt driven to soothe that dark spiral of emotional pain with booze. It was getting harder and harder to stay in that numb place I would often retreat to. The Jack and Coke was flowing now and I filled myself to the brim with Jack and Coke so I could land the punches with no inhibitions. Billy drove me to her house, and I hid behind a tree in her front yard as he knocked on the door and casually asked for her. When she came to the door, I jumped out from behind the tree and yelled at her to come and fight me. I am sure she was shocked that Billy, her brothers' best friend, and who had been her lover, was now bringing his wife to fight her. She walked down the steps, and we instantly lit into each other, but it was probably more comical than anything because I was so drunk. It descended quickly into a hair-pulling contest that ended in a very anticlimactic way. I am certain we looked like two staggering junior highers. I thought to myself, though, that she'd be stupid to go back to him after this. I also made a vow to myself to be more aware of the females in my life, and not always be so trusting.

Heading South with Scars

Billy had moved back in with Mindy and me at this point, and I wanted him there despite all that had occurred. We both wanted to make it work. Our apartment was just a few blocks from Muncie Central High School. We walked everywhere together, as we didn't have a car. We saw a stroller sitting outside of a house with a for sale sign of two dollars on it. We took the stroller and left an IOU note, hoping that the owners would understand. Several days later we went back and introduced ourselves, paying them the two dollars we owed. One day we walked across town to Samantha's house, Danny's mom, because she wanted us to see the new place she'd moved into. When we arrived, though, her boyfriend Kevin did not want anyone there. Instead, we went next door to her brother's house, and Billy started drinking with him. Soon Kevin came over in a drunken stupor picking fights with everyone. Kevin was a mean alcoholic with only one eye. Billy demanded that he calm down. Billy had been bullied most of his life and now took things way too far when it came to fighting. He would overreact and push things to the max when it came to starting fights. Swiftly, with a shocking twist of his arm, Kevin thrust a knife deep in Billy's left bicep inches from his heart, and instantly they were in a violent brawl.

Kevin taunted Billy with his knife as they circled the house ominously. Billy ran after him in a rage and found him at his place, where he attacked him with a two-by-four he had found. We started walking home and realized we needed to get Billy to the hospital as soon as possible. We arrived at the hospital for the stab wound, and Kevin arrived later in much worse shape. The police questioned Billy, and he made up a story about what had happened. The week progressed and Billy grew more and more anxious that Kevin was going to press charges. The thought of being arrested motivated him to consider moving us to Orlando, Florida, where Abby and her boyfriend, plus several other friends, had moved to. They were doing well, they had told us, and without further thought we made plans within a couple of hours to move to the Sunshine State to join them.

We lived by the seat of our pants, like two feathers blowing in the wind, with no real direction or plan. We found a car someone was going to junk and bought it for $75. We packed it up tight and took off for Orlando. We didn't have cell phones at that time, and they didn't have a landline either, so there was no way to tell them we were coming. We stopped in Indianapolis and talked to Jimmy, Abby's brother, and convinced him to come along. While we were filling up the car after picking up Jimmy, Billy had to hotwire the brake lights to make them work, and manually touch them together when we made a stop. Suddenly, police cars surrounded us in a tangle of chaotic lights and sirens. They questioned the guys, pressing for information. My mind was reeling, thinking if they found the gun under the seat we would not be going anywhere! A man from the gas station ran out and informed the officers that it wasn't us they were looking for, and in an instant, they were gone.

I want you to picture us in a tiny hatchback bomb of a car, Billy and Jimmy in the front seat and Mindy and me in the back seat with a mountain of scattered belongings and clothes. We were stuffed in this car like sardines. We limped along in our disposable car and showed up unannounced on their doorstep. I remember the surprise on their faces when we told them we were there to move in. Looking back, I can't believe we showed up this way, but they graciously opened their small one-bedroom house to us, and soon there were three couples, two single guys, one baby, and a pit bull all living together in that one-bedroom house. Nine people in a very small house infested with fleas and a pit bull. We were in a tight spot, and I know they didn't really want us there. It wasn't a good arrangement for anyone. We were basically all on top of each other, with no privacy. When we arrived in Florida, we had twenty dollars to our name. I was desperate enough to call my dad to see if he would loan us some money to get us through the next couple of weeks. I had made it a point in my life to never ask my dad for anything except for the $180 to rent my wedding dress and Billy's tux for our wedding. I purposely asked for the least amount of money as possible. Billy and I went down to the pay phone to make the call. I called collect, and he accepted. I told him our situation and asked if he could loan us anything; he refused. The anger I felt toward my father for his perpetual abandonment continued to build inside of me. However, I stuffed it down, never allowing it to surface.

With my father. I never responded to his refusal to help us with disrespect or going off on him. I would simply stuff it all down, and I responded with, "Okay, Dad. We're so sorry to have bothered you. Love you," and moved on.

I don't know how we made it. Billy found a job, and us three women were hired at the concession stand of the Wet 'n Wild water park, which is now Volcano Bay. We could get in for free for being an employee there, and with the scorching Florida sun that was a wonderful perk. I remember that my self-esteem was very low when we went to apply at the waterpark. They were hiring lifeguards, and I was a certified lifeguard, but I applied for the less paying job. I don't know why I did that, but I believe it was because I simply didn't think I deserved the better paying job. I was filled with self-contempt. It quickly became obvious that we hadn't thought this situation through, so after only six weeks we decided to return to Indiana. We went to visit my mom upon our return and stayed there for several days. She and Austin had not been getting along as usual and had a huge blow-up while we were there. She went into a rage not only with Austin, but with Billy and me. She exploded telling all of us that she hated us and wanted us all to leave. Billy and I talked things over, and we decided that we would ask my dad if Mindy and I could stay with him for a few weeks until Billy went to Muncie, got a job, and found a place for us to stay. I knew that if he said yes, Mindy and I would be staying with my stepmom and it would be a hard month, but I also knew that would be better than for us to be homeless, couch surfing until we were able to get our own place. It took everything I had to ask him. My stomach twisted into an anxious knot just thinking about it. He turned us down.

With my dad leaving me with no other choice we asked Austin if he wanted to come back with us to Muncie, even though we didn't have a place to stay—we were basically homeless. Austin needed to leave the situation with Mom as much as she did. We contacted my Aunt Brenda and Uncle David, asking them to allow us to stay with them for a few days, and they agreed. The four of us tumbled into their home in exhaustion. Austin got a job soon after and was sent out of state. Hard times come and go, and in between those spaces you keep on living and loving.

During this time, I had missed several periods and knew I was a couple months' pregnant. The next day I began to have very bad cramps and asked Billy to take me to the hospital. In the car, I began spotting blood and felt the urgent need to get there as quickly as we could. We were ushered into an emergency room and waited for the doctor to come in. When he finally appeared, carelessly flipping through my chart, he asked me what seemed to be the problem. I told him I was pregnant and that I'd been cramping and spotting blood and was worried about the baby. Then came the words that will always stay with me: "How do you know you're pregnant?"

I looked at him and shook my head and said, "Because I know I am." He asked if I'd taken a pregnancy test, and I shook my head no. He looked up slowly, centering his eyes right on mine, and said, "Then you can't know that you are pregnant, can you?" My brain didn't want to register how he was treating me, like a small insect to be brushed away.

"Can you give me one?" I pleaded. "I know I'm pregnant and am afraid that I'm having a miscarriage. Please help me." He shook his head, already heading toward the curtain, and said no and told me to go to a place in Muncie that gave free pregnancy tests, adding, "We can't help you at all until you do." I know that he could have given me a pregnancy test and chose not to. He sent me away as I was cramping and bleeding.

I was horror-stricken and looked at Billy, who was just as upset. I had been treated as a low-class citizen because I was young and looked like I didn't have money. Didn't I deserve treatment too? We left quickly and went to get the free pregnancy test as fast as we could, where they helped us and confirmed that I was pregnant. We returned to my aunt and uncle's house, where I lay down to try and rest, to stave off what was happening to my body. I got up some time later to get a drink of water in the kitchen, and as I did, I felt a warm gush of water run down the inside of my legs. My water had broken.

The ambulance was called, and they picked me up and took me back to the same hospital that hours before had refused to help me. In the emergency room, they told me I had lost the baby. I was inconsolable and furious. They wheeled me away for a D&C, and when I came out of the procedure, I was devastated that I had just lost our baby and that a doctor would turn me away in a time of desperation. He had taken one look at me and judged me someone not worthy of care. I will never forget the loss of our baby and the treatment we received.

BEAUTIFULLY UNBROKEN

BILLY MARY AND OUR NIECE TALISA UNNAMED NIECE AND OUR
DAUGHTER MINDY

CHAPTER 16

SWAT Raid

Billy worked for my Uncle David, and we scraped enough money together to rent an efficiency apartment at which the rent was due weekly. We were only there a couple of weeks before we had to move out, as we couldn't afford it. We moved in with a friend at a notorious party house, twenty-four hours a day, the place to lose yourself in drugs and alcohol. Desperation leads you down many roads, and we had been down many and lost ourselves on some. Several weeks after we moved in, our friend moved out, and we took over renting the little shotgun house that sat forlornly on a side street. We sold marijuana to make the rent, a parade of known felons and criminals coming and going. There was violence and fighting, yet I tried to make it a home to my little family the best way I knew how.

While in Florida our motor had blown up in our disposable car, and Billy's boss had sold us an older but nicer car with air conditioning that we had brought back from Orlando. Now Billy began to allow friends to use it, and we both knew eventually that they were using it for burglaries. Why did we do this? This was our life, and when from a child you are conditioned that partying, stealing, drugs, and violence are normal, you just accept that lifestyle. It's all you have known! We'd seen much worse, so how could it hurt? When our friends would come back and drop the car off, the trunk would be loaded with stolen goods like knickknacks and bundles of gold-plated utensils. They asked us if we would like to buy some of it. At first Billy was hesitant, thinking he shouldn't do it, but then he called them back and said he did want to buy some of it. They began to store some of the stolen goods in our house, and while I felt a tad uneasy, I let them leave it there.

All the partying that went on at our house brought out many different characters, and one of them was a man who had just gotten out of prison after doing ten to fifteen years. We were trusting, as we had once been without places to sleep, and let him stay on our couch, which in retrospect was a very bad idea. Along with letting this man sleep in our home, a series of shootings had been going on in our neighborhood, a kind of gang rivalry of sorts. One of our friends had stolen some pot and a gun from some drug dealers. At the time, I didn't consider us to be drug dealers because in my mind it was just pot, something I had done since I was nine years old. But the rival group thought differently and wouldn't let it stand.

Shots Fired

One evening I was sitting outside with Mindy on the front step of our little house. The evening was dusky, and I took in the brisk air and exhaled as my baby and I quieted ourselves in play. She was beautiful, our little girl, and I loved her so much. Suddenly a car came by slowly and shots were fired in our direction. I saw the flaring light as the bullets left the gun. I couldn't see well as it was nearly dark outside. The sound of bullets whizzing over the top of my head sent me diving to the ground. I grabbed Mindy in a panicked frenzy and screamed as several more shots tore into the house and I scrambled inside for cover.

Billy flew down the hallway to see if we were okay. I was so rattled and couldn't believe what had just happened. We were fine—we checked Mindy from head to toe—but Billy was incensed. He knew who had done it and set out on his bike to find them. Billy found the guy and questioned him. He denied having anything to do with it. Right there in the middle of the street Billy started fist fighting him, and the police came and separated them and sent both men on their way. I couldn't shake the unsettled feeling I had, and we were both on edge. Billy was looking over his shoulder and out the windows all the time, afraid that the rival gang was going to come back or, even worse, bring reinforcements. All of this for being associated with the guy who stole a gun and weed from them.

One day not long afterward, in September, I was in the house with Mindy and two friends Becky and Lisa who had skipped school to hang out with me. Mindy was in her walker, happy and moving around the room. We were all smoking pot and talking, the room filled with a smoky haze. Now I am appalled that we didn't seem to realize that if we were getting high off pot, so was Mindy from the secondhand smoke! But those thoughts didn't enter our minds then. Billy had recently started a new job on a tree-cutting crew, but rain had moved in and he was sent home early. The man we had let sleep on our couch, Larry, came in and said he wanted to buy some weed. Billy told him we didn't have any and that he would need to go next door where our dealer lived. He'd been acting shifty, enough for me to take notice of it, but I dismissed the thought as quickly as it had come. He left and Billy announced that he was going to take a bath. I turned my head and took another toke of the joint, letting it blow softly out of my mouth. I could faintly hear dogs barking behind the house as I turned my head back to my friends and the conversation we were having.

BANG! BANG! The loudest sound I had ever heard was coming from the back of the house, and I whipped my eyes to the back door, which was suddenly lying on the floor of the hallway. Confused, I looked up to see men with shotguns storming into our home dressed in all black with masks covering their faces, screaming, "TAKE COVER! TAKE COVER!" A scream started deep inside me and hurtled out as piercing as a knife. Mindy was crying and chaos reigned as they overtook the rooms inside the house.

"Get down! Get down!" they ordered gruffly. I could see they had Billy on the floor of the kitchen, with no shirt on, and just his cut-off blue jean shorts, arms behind his back in handcuffs. He was lying on top of broken glass that the invaders had shattered in their raid. They moved into the front room where we were and roughly herded my friends out, then Billy, and finally me, with Mindy in my arms. She was wailing and upset because I was. She had no idea what had upset her tiny world, and at first neither did I. I knew then, though, that a SWAT team had invaded our home and turned our world upside down.

As I walked out, I looked up and down the street and realized what a big operation this had been. The street had been blocked off, and ambulances and police cars were everywhere. SWAT guys crouched on the roofs of the houses pointing down at us with their shotguns. My heart raced uncontrollably as I held Mindy tightly, and right there on the front porch they started asking me questions.

"Who sold you the drugs?"

"Where did you get the stolen goods?"

"Did you know about the burglaries?"

I stood stock still, listening to the sound of my heartbeat, and knowing that this wasn't going to end well. We had devised a plan that if anything like this ever happened, I was to give the answers I had memorized like the alphabet I learned in grammar school. But as I rattled off the answers and names Billy and I had talked about; I knew they were falling on deaf ears. They knew I was lying, and their frustration built into an angry tirade. They threatened to take my baby away from me and put her into foster care. I looked at the detective and realized it was the same one who had tried to help me, the detective who gave me a tour of the juvenile detention center and told me to straighten up, the same one who had taken me from Danny's house when I was on the run.

"We're going to give you one more chance, Jodie," he said. "Tell us where you got the stolen property from." I battled within myself, knowing that since I was nine years old it had been ingrained in me not to snitch, not to give away what you knew. My life and all that had been programmed into me won out over reason and common sense. I don't think it really registered in my head what the actual consequences were going to be. Detective Logan looked at me holding Mindy and said, "Jodie, I wish you would have straightened up." He then pried Mindy from my arms, as I was crying, put her in a car, and drove away.

Game Over

The devastation I felt couldn't be measured at that moment. There was no disengaging from my emotions and escaping to a safer place that day. Despair. Sadness. Fear. Emptiness. Regret. Panic. They had taken my baby! I was at my lowest as they handcuffed me and tucked my head into a car that Billy had been forced into as well. They drove us to the police station where we were interrogated even further, neither one of us giving up the information they wanted. It wasn't long before we figured out that Larry, the man who had been staying with us, had snitched. We found out he'd gotten in trouble for something, and they had forced his hand to wear a wire to get information on us so he could be let off.

Because we wouldn't give them the answers they wanted, they put Mindy in temporary foster care. They refused to tell us where she was, and it was the most painful thing I have ever experienced. My stomach clenched into an anguished knot as I tried to silence the terror I felt inside. I wanted to see if they would let us out by the next day, by bail, and hoped we would be able to get Mindy back, but it was not to be. The next morning we were taken from the jail, dirty and disheveled from the day before, and led to a small room where the welfare department also interrogated us. They treated us like scumbags, and in their eyes we were nothing more than abusive, drug-pushing thieves. They determined that along with having known felons in the house and dealing in stolen property, the environment we'd created for our daughter was one of chaos and neglect. We were young and so immature, but Mindy had always been fed and cared for. I came from a life of chaos as well and had been doing the best I knew how to do. They told us they were taking our daughter from us and putting her in foster care, then ushered us back to jail. I lowered my head and felt rage at my choices and what they had led us to; all hope shattered, but I vowed I would get my baby back no matter what.

The next day we had to appear before a judge where a few procedural happenings took place for the stolen property charges and arrest. There wasn't a whole lot happening at this procedure, and I felt helpless to know what I should be doing. They told us they were going to place us back in jail until they could figure out what they were going to do. All I could think about was my baby. *Where is she? Is she crying? She must feel so scared and alone. What kind of people have her? What if they hurt her?*

As they were leading me back to the court house holding cell for prisoners I looked over and saw the Sheriff's office, I broke free from the guard and ran into the sheriff's office where I pleaded desperately with the Sheriff to hear my story. I hadn't been raised through the life I lived to be afraid to take a chance on something that meant everything. The deputy tried to stop me, but the sheriff held up his hand and told me I could talk to him. I poured out the story of our arrest and also telling him how much we loved our daughter and cared for her. I told him that though we hadn't made the wisest choices and were immature parents, we had always taken care of her. She was fed, clothed, and loved beyond measure—even though our actions showed otherwise. We had never neglected her.

I think back to what must have been going through his head when I bolted into his office. And to this day I'm not sure what made him release us on our own recognizance, but he did! We went to stay with a friend that night, as we didn't want to stay in the raid house. We were so happy to be out, but that was soon shattered when our lawyer called to say we had to appear in court again the next day for our official ar-raignment. These proceedings were matter of fact, set in stone, and we were put back in a cell afterwards with bail set at six thousand dollars. My dad and Billy's mom and stepdad came to bail us out. After all the many times my dad wasn't there—wouldn't help me or provide for my most basic needs—now he came to help bail me out of jail. I was thankful.

After we were bailed out, it was a few days before we contacted the welfare office, we were numb from all that had happened and did not know what to do. Once we contacted them we were given a time and date to visit her. We could not wait to see our baby girl. One week later we were ushered into an upstairs room at the welfare office and told to wait until they brought her in. I had bought a disposable camera so I could take some pictures of her, and I held it in my hand wondering how life had brought me to this juncture. The people in the welfare office were cold to us, almost to the point that I couldn't bear to be in their presence. We waited, and suddenly the door opened, and a woman walked in holding Mindy. She reached for us and my heart burst into a million pieces as we just held her, loved her. I wanted to hold on to her forever. Her smell, her smile, her little dimples… It ripped my heart to shreds thinking of having to let her go. When they took her away from me, I looked at Billy, and we vowed that we would do everything in our power to dig ourselves out of this life.

JODIE BALLENGER

THE MUNCIE STAR NEWSPAPER REPORTED//Tuesday September 13, 1988

Four suspects in drug, burglary ring are arrested by city police

Four persons were arrested Monday by detectives who said they are trying to break up a drug and burglary ring and stop a series of street shootings over the past month.

The suspects have been warring with each other and others over an apparent narcotic rip off, according to Ireland. The battle has been punctuated by a series of street shootings all over the city's southwest side over the past month. Two persons have been wounded by shotgun blast so far, and a third man suffered a gunshot wound in his knee, Ireland said.

THE MUNCIE STAR NEWSPAPER REPORTED // Wednesday September 14,1988

Four Nabbed in Raid; Two Remain in Jail

Members of the Indiana Law Enforcement Emergency Response Team and city detectives served warrants at three different addresses near the downtown area. The response

• 222 •

team was activated because police had learned some of those they intended to arrest might be armed.

Police served warrants at both Fifth Street residences and a vacant apartment building in the 100 block of West Willard Street. The Willard Street building is about a block northeast of the two apartments raided. Police said property reported stolen in at least six burglaries was recovered in the raids.

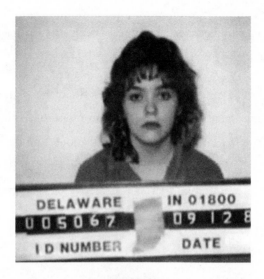

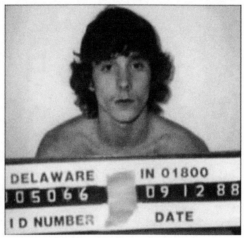

OUR MUG SHOTS AFTER THE RAID

OUR FIRST VISIT WITH MINDY AFTER SHE WAS PLACED IN FOSTER
CARE

CHAPTER 17

Homeless in Indy

As we waited for our jury trial, we found an upstairs apartment and Billy got a job as a dishwasher at a restaurant. I was a waitress at the same restaurant. It was a beginning. Mindy spent thirty days in foster care and every single day of that time was agonizing to me when I thought about her. That little face was so trusting. I felt like I'd let her down. We worked hard to get enough money to make a home for her so we could get her back, no matter what the trial would bring. After thirty days in foster care, they allowed Mindy to stay with Billy's mom. We were very happy about this but wanted her back.

We asked the welfare department, "What can we do to get her back?" We went to parenting classes, completing them successfully after fifteen weeks. They told us we needed our own apartment with a separate room for Mindy, so we got one ready in our upstairs apartment. We set it up with all the things you would need to take care of a baby, down to the tiniest details. The welfare department came to do a check, and after poking around for a while haphazardly, shook their heads no.

They now told us that part of getting her back would involve getting a comprehensive mental health evaluation and drug tests for each of us. We started seeing a counselor who asked us questions on drug use: How much? What kind? Do you still do it now? She even asked us how much tea we drank a day. She asked us heavy questions on if we'd done cocaine or other substances. Billy had never done cocaine and told her so. She looked at him and said, "Mr. Ballenger, every nineteen-year-old has done cocaine." Billy was furious because she didn't believe him, and he tried to walk out. She told him that if he walked away he would be viewed as not cooperating. The next visit we were told we would need to take a drug test. During the drug test, he knew he'd smoked marijuana and didn't want them to know he had it in his system, so he tampered with the test by diluting it in cold toilet water. When he handed it to the nurse, she had a startled look on her face because it was a cold urine sample.

We had a lot of time before our court date and needed a fresh start after all this frustration and bending over backward trying to please the authorities. I felt like we were on a hamster wheel, spinning infinitely and never able to get off. Just after

Christmas, Billy's mom said we could stay with her in Franklin, Indiana, for two weeks. She had Mindy, and we wanted to be with our daughter so much that we ached. She had turned one year old a little more than a month before, and Mary held a birthday party for her at her house. Mindy, her sweet little face covered with cake and smiles, had no idea what had befallen her world. We didn't want her to know.

I found a job working at a United gas station while we stayed at his mom's house. I felt lucky to have located this job in between being arrested and our trial. But when the two weeks were up, Billy's mom told us we had to leave; she'd meant business when she said two weeks. We didn't have a place to stay, and this meant we were out on the street with only our car to sleep in. For several weeks, we moved from parking lot to parking lot, taking showers in truck stops around Indianapolis. Sometimes we would be awakened by a strong flashlight being shone in our eyes by the police. We always told them we were on our way to Muncie and needed to stop for a rest. Then we would drive to another parking lot and fall back asleep. We were homeless, but at least I had a job.

Tricked

We lived our life moment by moment, knowing that we were deep in a pit that could swiftly take us under. It was a pit of our own making. I wanted to see light at the end of the tunnel, and when I think about those days sleeping in the car, I wonder how I didn't lose all the hope I may have once had. But we pressed on. Fighting for Mindy drove us both! In between those hazy days of moving our car around and working, Billy was told he needed to go in for a drug evaluation at the Richmond State Hospital. We were sure it had something to do with him tampering with a drug test he had taken earlier. When he arrived at Richmond State Hospital, he told them he was there for a drug evaluation, but they said, "No, you're here for drug treatment."

Billy couldn't believe they had tricked him and knew that everything about the way they'd gotten him there was not on the up and up. He told them after two days that he didn't belong there—that he was going to leave—but one of the counselors said to him, "Isn't your daughter worth it?" Billy knew anything he had to do for Mindy would be worth it. He became a model patient, cooperating and doing everything they wanted him to do. He was there for his twentieth birthday.

After thirty-six days he was released, and I went to pick him up. They still wouldn't let us have our daughter back. We began to believe they wouldn't give her back to us until after the trial, after they knew what the outcome would be. We were jumping through hoops because we were desperate for our baby and felt manipulated and tricked at everything we were made to do. The welfare department was cold and heartless to us, and instead of helping us they led us on. It felt nothing short of cruel.

After I received a check from working at the gas station, we found a cute house in the Fountain Square area of Indianapolis—a nice ranch-style home with a large kitchen and a small front and back yard. It was a place to call our own. After living on the streets, it felt like heaven had come down and made a place just for us. It was an unfurnished house, so we needed everything. Since my arrest I had called my dad, and he bailed me out of jail and was there for me. I was grateful that he was there for me when I really needed him this time. I called him and told him that we had rented a house and did not have any furniture. I also let him know Billy was in rehab. My dad and stepmom drove up that next weekend with a truckload of everything we needed. Furniture for our living room, including a TV, a queen-size bed and dresser for our room, a crib for Mindy, towels, washcloths, a coffee pot, hot plate, and a highchair. I am sure there were other things as well. My stepmom was showing me a side of herself I had not seen since I was a little girl before she married my dad. They also brought food. We were so grateful to them for being there for us in such a time of need. To this day, thinking back at this memory reduces me to tears. The stuffed anger I felt toward my dad's neglect and abandonment receded considerably. No words are adequate to thank them enough for being there for us during this time.

This allowed us to fix up a room for Mindy in case they would relent and let her come back to us. We regularly went to Billy's mom's house to see Mindy. His mom could see that we were changing our ways and that being without our baby had affected us greatly. She saw each thing we were trying desperately to do to win her back and felt sympathy for us. Even though she hadn't let us continue to stay at her home, she decided to allow Mindy to come and stay with us. The court system did not know this, and if they had it would've spelled more trouble for us. But they never found out, and we were as happy as three peas in a pod.

When Billy did his stint in drug rehab, I continued to work at the gas station where I had been trained as assistant manager. I also worked at McDonald's, getting up at 5 a.m. to work until 12:30 p.m. From there I would head to the gas station and work from 1 p.m. until 11 at night. I had to keep busy and my mind off Billy being in rehab and Mindy being with her grandma during this time, so I thought the best thing for me to do was to work as much as I could to save some money.

The gas station was at 71st and Keystone on the north side of town. It wasn't a bad section of town, and yet I had been robbed at gunpoint twice by the time Billy got out. I just gave them what they wanted and went about my work. I'd seen so much in my lifetime that I knew to just give them what they wanted. It didn't make it any less scary, and Billy told me that if I was ever robbed again, I had to quit the job; my safety was his priority.

Not long after Billy got out of rehab, I was robbed again. A man shoved a gun in my face demanding money from the cash register. I gave him what he wanted and with my heart racing knew that this was the end of the road. I called my boss, and he showed up and followed me home because he wanted to talk to Billy. He'd told me I was such a good worker and he couldn't afford to lose me. I told him that I didn't know what Billy would say. When he followed me home, he came inside and said to Billy, "I sure hope you won't make Jodie quit because I really need her."

Billy looked at me questioningly, and I nodded my head.

"She's been robbed again," my boss told him.

Billy got up and said, "That's it, she's quitting. She's done tonight. We'll be in tomorrow to get her check." And that was that.

I had lived my life on the edge, always unsure of what the next day may bring. Having to quit my job was just one more thing, and I took it in stride. I didn't know there was something, someone, out there orchestrating and pulling the tiny strings that connected my life. The loose ends were slowly being gathered up and knit back together, even as the future seemed murky. Billy and I went to the gas station the next morning to collect my check. It hadn't been delivered yet, so we waited around, a little impatient but knowing we must.

Glimmer of Hope

I saw a man come in the door, one I knew from coming in for gas over the past weeks, and he asked if he could get some water. He said his radiator was overheating. I went and filled up a small container for him then told him that I had been robbed at gunpoint again the evening before. He couldn't believe it had happened again then went out the door to take care of his vehicle. It wasn't long before he came back in and said, "That is the strangest thing. When I went to fill that radiator tank with water it was completely full. It's not overheated at all, but I knew I had to stop here."

We chatted a little longer about the robbery until Billy said to me, "Jodie, I have to go. I need to find a job." My check still hadn't arrived, and I wasn't sure what to do.

The man overheard our conversation and said, "Do you need a job?" Billy nodded his head, and I felt a shiver go through me as the man answered, "I do construction work. I'll hire you right here. I need a helper." They shook hands and Billy had a job. Just like that. He said to us, "My name is Jeff and my wife's name is Dianna."

He invited us to church on Easter with him and his wife, and once he saw my interest in going, he boldly asked, "Do you mind if we come over to your house tonight to talk for a little while? We'd love to tell you about our church." I had been wanting to try going back to a church, something inside me yearning for more, and I told him so. We looked at each other feeling a bit unsure, but this man had hired Billy without a second thought—what would be the harm? We agreed.

Later that evening, after I had finally retrieved my check, Jeff and Dianna came over with their little girl Erica, who was a couple months older than Mindy. Since we didn't yet have a kitchen table, Dianna and I sat on the floor in the kitchen. Billy and Jeff were in the living room getting to know each other, and the two girls played on the living room floor and in Mindy's room. Billy was to report for work the next day, and I could hear them in the other room—Jeff telling Billy all about the church they were attending several blocks away from us. Billy said we'd dreamed of going to one with stained-glass windows and a service that lasted for one hour, and right afterward going out to lunch. Normal, everyday things. Billy told him we didn't want to attend a loud church, and Jeff gave Billy a verse from the Bible about David dancing before the Lord.

Dianna was so easy to talk to. I didn't know at the time that she was witnessing to me—telling me of God's love and His plans for me. It wasn't long before she told me about the rapture and the second coming of Christ, and as she spoke I felt an urgency rise within me that I had never felt before.

"Are you saved, Jodie?" she asked, looking me right in the eyes.

I didn't know if I was because I didn't really know what it all meant. I told her I had gone to church while I was at White's reform school, but I wasn't sure if I was saved. I grew a bit nervous and half expected Jesus to appear right there in my kitchen while we were sitting on the floor! I needed to get this thing done and accept Jesus into my heart right then because what if I missed out on the rapture? I wanted to rededicate my life immediately, and I couldn't get her to speak fast enough. She gently explained it all to me then led me in this prayer:

> "Heavenly Father, I have sinned against You. I want forgiveness for all my sins. I believe that Jesus died on the cross for me and rose again. Father, I give You my life to do with as You wish. I want Jesus Christ to come into my life and my heart."

Did I expect the room to light up and be filled with a heavenly light? Maybe not, but I knew I had a lot to learn and that this was a start. I had spent my entire life doing what I wanted, living for myself, and here was a chance to make it right, to do something good. They invited us to attend a Wednesday night service the next day, and they left with us promising to be there. I knew Billy felt obligated to go, as he'd been given a job out of nowhere, but I was hoping this would take us down the road we needed to go. With the trial coming up, I felt an uneasiness inside of me, and what our new friends had shown and offered gave us a hopeful purpose.

We didn't have dressy clothes to wear to church. We had just come from being homeless in Indianapolis and our wardrobe was sorely lacking, so we went down to the thrift store and picked out some things for Wednesday evening. As we approached the church, walking down the street, we saw that it was a little bitty church. And when we entered, it was everything we weren't sure we wanted in a church. It was loud and rollicking, with people running and praising God up and down the aisles, and music so loud it shook the rafters.

We stood rather stunned at the back of the church, feeling chills all over. Jeff and Dianna saw us and invited us to sit down front, which is not what we wanted to do. We were so uncomfortable! It felt like little needles pricking us all over. A desire to run out of there welled up inside both of us. Tambourines were rattling and people were dancing, and throughout a series of calls to the men, they all went to the front of the church to dance before the Lord. Billy was the only man to stay seated, refusing to put himself in such an awkward predicament. We both sat rooted to our seats and in utter shock.

After the evening was over, we walked out and said we were never going back there again—it was too weird for us. They asked if we had plans for Easter Sunday, saying, "Would you please come to our worship service?" We agreed and found ourselves there yet again. Each time we went we would say that we were never coming back, that we couldn't handle the style of worship. I believe the reason we kept going back was because Billy didn't want to lose the job, even though Jeff never would have fired him for not coming to church. He wasn't that kind of man. Yet it wasn't long before Billy found himself playing tambourine up front, and we sought more and more answers to the questions we had.

Billy worked diligently for Jeff on his construction crew, and it felt good to have steady money coming in. One day at work, Billy asked Jeff about the strange language he had heard people speaking in the church, wondering if it might be Hebrew. Jeff chuckled and explained about speaking in tongues and that it was a gift from God to receive. One Sunday they had an altar call, and I felt nudged to go up front. Right there, I re-dedicated my life to God. Billy rededicated his life as well, but he didn't leave his seat.

We continued to attend church and had long since confided in Jeff and Diana about our plight and the upcoming court date. They were the only ones at church that we told, and they prayed for us and the outcome incessantly, to the point that I felt maybe there was hope for us. But we lied; we told them we didn't do it. Being brand-new Christians, we didn't grasp the concept yet of being truthful. I had lied my way through situations my whole life. The pastor of the church, we found out, was a deputy sheriff in Indianapolis. We had wanted to confide in him about our trial, but when we found out he was a deputy sheriff, we didn't want him to think we were only attending so we could gain his trust for help. We never met with him. The night before our court date, I was baptized. After weeks of attending this tiny church our day in court had come.

MINDY'S FIRST BIRTHDAY PARTY

CHAPTER 18

Judge, Jury,
and Half a Chance

I was nervous. Who wouldn't be? I wanted to believe in all that we had been taught in recent weeks, to lay down our burdens and let Jesus carry them for us. It was a hard thing to believe that someone would care enough about us to do that. My newfound trust in a person I couldn't see was a tenuous thing, but we prayed together and believed that we wouldn't go to jail. We spent some quiet time with Mindy that morning before dropping her off at Abby's house to babysit and heading to the courthouse.

This was a jury trial, and we were tried together in the same courtroom. The first day passed as all the information was given and dissected, the back and forth of it full of anxiety-inducing minutes. The state-appointed lawyer gave our version of the story, and we could only sit and listen as the process moved forward. We went home that evening hoping against hope we wouldn't be found guilty, and not feeling good about our chances. The next morning, we went back and sat in the courtroom knowing that whatever was said there would change the direction of our lives. I thought back to all the things I had gone through in my life, first as a child and now as a wife with a baby. I was still a child, had never had a moment to be a child in my world of madness and chaos. Random memories flashed before my eyes as I thought back to my mom and dad, my stepmom's fury, and Austin's kindness. Every single second of my life ran through my mind it seemed, yet I knew that with all that had befallen me, in the end, I had made my own choices to do good or bad.

The jury deliberated only a few hours, and when they came back and handed the judge the verdict, I closed my eyes and breathed a short prayer. When I opened them, I was standing up alongside Billy, watching the judge's lips move slowly: Count one, guilty. Count two, guilty. Count three, guilty. We were found guilty on all three Class D felonies, for receiving stolen property. My knees wanted to buckle, and I looked at Billy pleadingly as they whisked us away from each other. Billy was put in jail in Muncie, and I was taken to the Portland jail because Muncie was building a new jail and didn't have a long-term place to put me, to await sentencing. I couldn't believe what had just happened. Somebody called Billy's mom and informed her that we had been found guilty.

It was arranged for her to pick up Mindy at Abby's and care for her until we found out what our sentence would be.

When I went back to court for my sentencing several weeks later, I saw Billy and wanted to cry. I missed my husband, I missed my baby, and I missed the freedom that had been snatched away from us. We stood in front of the judge, praying she would go easy on us. The prosecutor recommended six months for me and twelve years for Billy with the part he played in receiving the stolen property. I was thinking to myself there was no way she would give us more than probation or maybe six months in jail. But life doesn't always deal the hand you want.

CHAPTER 19

Prison

Judge Betty Shelton Cole handed down her sentence. Count one, two years. Count two, two years. Count three, two years, to be served consecutively. She sentenced us both to six years in the Indiana Department of Corrections. It hit me like a ton of bricks. I could not believe we were going to prison for possession of stolen property. My feet wouldn't walk, couldn't walk. I was dragged out of the courtroom and put back in jail until they could transport me to the Indiana Women's Prison.

Hysteria washed over me like a tidal wave as I mentally replayed all the things I could have done differently. Suddenly, the dysfunctional and flawed choices we had made glared at me like Vegas show beacons. But we could not go back for a "do-over"; we could not undo all the many defective decisions we had made that had painfully piled up to bring us to this place in our lives. I was the only woman being held at the jail. It was a horrible place. The worst part of my time at this jail was the detestable food. Jail food is never great. Soup was on the menu one day, and as usual my meal was passed to me through a slot in the steel door. When I sat down and dipped my spoon into the bowl, I could see what looked like tiny dark things floating in the broth. On closer inspection, I could see that it was bugs; I had been served bug soup. BUG SOUP! My stomach recoiled, nausea sweeping over me.

After a week in this facility, I was transferred to the Indiana Women's Prison, the same one where I had gone through the Scared Straight program when I was thirteen years old. I was in shock, fear filling me like a cold, metal fist in my stomach. The women had gotten in my face when I went through that program. They had verbally assaulted and jeered me, telling me they would find me if I ever had to come there. "You don't want to come here," one woman screamed, "because if you do I'll find you and make you my own!" I knew what that meant. I would have to fight my way through this sentence. I was praying to God that none of them recognized me after all these years, and here I was, entering the women's prison at the age of nineteen. Despair surrounded me like an oppressive fog.

The Indiana Women's Prison sits just a few miles from downtown Indianapolis. I sat in the back seat of the police car, silent, all the way there. When the police car pulled up to the prison, I saw massive brick buildings surrounded by towering fences with sharp barbed wire at the top. As we entered, a gate opened with a loud, echoing screech and then closed behind us with a resounding bang. The deputy gruffly escorted me to the intake office where a stern corrections officer asked me a series of probing questions. Next, I was taken to a room where I was made to strip, squat down, and cough. They gave me a blue prison uniform and my bedding then walked me upstairs to diagnostics. I was taken to the cell at the very end of the hall and ordered to put my bedding in it. What came next was a humiliating shower where I was doused with a white powder used to kill lice. All inmates had to go through the same procedure. I was given another blue uniform to put on and walked back to my four-by-eight cell.

I glanced forlornly at the two-steel bunkbed-style cots, one small desk and chair, a toilet in the corner open to the entire room, and a small window with a dismal view of the prison courtyard. I was ushered out at various times from this cell to be tested for diseases and different diagnostics. They evaluated our mental tests, to see if we were high security or low security and decided which prison we were to be sent to.

I was allowed to have a small portable TV no more than twelve inches wide. Since I was a brand-new Christian, I spent most of my time in my cell watching TBN, a Christian

TV channel. I would watch Paul and Jan Crouch and all their guests. This was a whole new way of life for me. I also tried to read my Bible, but in the beginning, it was so hard for me to understand. I am so thankful for Bible translations I can understand.

I was only released from that cell for one hour per day of recreation time. Of course, during rec time and the times we were together for meals, we all managed to find out what everyone was in for and how long their sentence was. Three times a day we would all line up to be marched over to the cafeteria to eat. I was in a state of constant hyper-vigilance, assessing my surroundings and staying alert to possible threats and danger.

Daily there would be new inmates in line for the cafeteria. After my first few days, I noticed a new inmate, about six feet tall with a solid masculine build, light brown boyish hair, and probably in her mid-twenties. She always cut in line either in front of me or behind me as we were lining up for the cafeteria. So, we sat together at meals and talked; her name was Jamie. She seemed nice, but one day at dinner she casually began to eat food right off my plate. My eyes widened in astonishment, but I said nothing. The advance was clear. It became obvious to me that she was attempting to recruit me into a relationship I did not welcome. I tried not to give off any vibes that would have attracted her to me. I knew then with settled certainty she desired more than friendship. I headed swiftly back to my cell, my heart rate increasing anxiously, knowing that if she tried to touch me I would just declare that I was straight and married with a child. However, I realized that might not make any difference to her.

At rec time that evening I sat down with three other women to play cards. Soon enough Jamie was there, pulling up a chair to sit right beside me. Suddenly, without warning, she brazenly grabbed my knee with a firm grip. I froze for a second, my breath catching in my lungs, then bolted up and into my self-protective mode.

"Hey!" I yelled. "I am married and have a child! I am straight!" I glared at her as she met my glare steadily.

She threw her hands up and declared, "That's all you needed to tell me, man!" She backed off and acquired a girlfriend by the end of rec time that night. I was relieved. I found out in one of our discussions over dinner when we first met that she was serving a very long sentence for murdering her girlfriend.

New girls were arriving daily, and one of them became my roommate. She was in for prostitution, and I found out that she lived in the neighborhood Billy and I had lived in— Fountain Square, only blocks from the women's prison. She was in her twenties and had been incarcerated there once before. We got along well. I was thankful for a roommate I didn't have to see as a threat. The stories she told me kept me entertained and helped distract me from the gloomy and oppressive atmosphere of the prison.

Soon I had to appear before the people who had tested me during orientation, and they told me what prison I would be staying in. You always hope for minimum security instead of max. This gives you more freedom, and the inmates are not quite as threatening. I was also given my DOC number: 893699. I had to memorize this number. After four weeks at the women's prison, I was moved to a women's cottage at the Indiana Girls' School—a minimum-security facility—where I served the remainder of my sentence. It was May 1989; I should have been graduating high school, but instead I was serving a six-year prison sentence.

When I arrived at the Indiana Girls' School, I wasn't sure what to expect. Anxiety brought my nerves into sharp focus as I tried to calm myself. What I'd experienced so far left no room for me to believe this place was any better. The school was laid out like a campus, with one building that housed the women. Long halls filled each resident building, and there were no locks on the doors. I didn't have a roommate at first and liked being alone to think on my situation and study more about God in the Bible. I was so new at learning about Him and didn't want to let what I had learned go; I craved more. I had begun to communicate with Him regularly in prayer as I went through my days, an ongoing dialogue. It gave me a measure of comfort and peace.

Corruption Inside

There were different places to work in this prison—crews for the powerhouse, lawn care, cafeteria, janitors for the school, janitors for the admission office, electrical and plumbing, and maintenance. For my work duty, I was put on a maintenance crew doing cleanup. All the crews had men supervisors; the crew supervisor, another female prisoner, and I made up this crew. We would meet in a small office to see what our duties were for the day, and it didn't take me long to discover what was going on with the two of them. They constantly flirted with each other, and he would ask me to leave the office. I knew they were having sex once I left the room. I did not want to get involved and told know one. This supervisor was married, and his wife worked across campus as a corrections officer for the girls who were locked up there. Three or four weeks later they were found out. She was sent back to the women's prison, and he was fired. How did authorities find out? You could not be in their presence and not pick up on the vibe that they were in a relationship.

• 249 •

I, however, was moved to a different crew at the powerhouse. This was where the prison got its power from, so it was an important part of the complex. Seven or so men worked here on a fixed basis, and five women inmates were assigned to this crew. Underneath the powerhouse was a grid of intricate tunnels that led to everywhere across campus. I noticed whenever I came to work that the girls on my crew would disappear at different times and reappear later with cigarettes, money, or drugs. It was happening here too: they were trading sexual favors with the men to gain something they needed and wanted. The men had everything available that would entice the women to do this. It didn't take much asking as everyone used each other for their own selfish gain. I kept my head down and all this information to myself as I just wanted to do my time without any drama and get out as soon as possible.

I was carrying my Bible around and studying God's Word every opportunity I had, and I wanted everyone around me to know it. I'm sure I was not pulled into that mess primarily because they were aware I spent all my extra time reading my Bible, which sent a clear signal to all that I was not interested in going into any tunnel with anyone. I did my job there, but they soon moved me again. This time I was placed in an administration building as part of the janitorial crew, where I could keep to myself and not worry about what others were doing. This was a huge relief. The drama in the prison was outrageous, and it wasn't just the prison mates instigating it. Eventually the things happening at the powerhouse were found out. The girls who had taken part in it were moved to a maximum-security prison, and several of the men were fired. They didn't fire them all, though. The perverted happenings continued on.

I worked in the administration building for a long time, and from eight to five every day there would be a job to do that kept me busy. I was thankful for this hard work to keep me doing something worthwhile and distracting. Soon I was promoted to the position of janitor in the girl's school on campus—it looked like a regular high school. As prisoners, we were not allowed to speak to the girls locked up there. This was a very firm, settled rule they would not bend on. I enjoyed this job, but it became an issue because the administrators and teachers there kept confusing me for a student. For at least the first two weeks people would stop and tell me to "get back to class," and every time I had to explain that I was an inmate from the women's prison and was doing the job assigned to me. I was at this job until around springtime when I was moved onto the lawn care crew. This, by far, was my favorite job while in prison. Most of the time I was able to work alone. There was a freedom in riding around on my little tractor, making straight lines in the grass. I could be alone and stay out of trouble, because that was my personal goal. It was a way for me to examine and evaluate my direction in life and the new things I had discovered in studying about Jesus. I still didn't know what He was all about, but I desperately wanted to.

Many times, while I was riding around tending the yards, I would think deeply on the words I had found in the Bible that didn't make sense to me yet. I wanted them to make sense and kept reading them, even when I wasn't sure what they meant. In my heart I felt certain these words were the path out of my former life of chaos, crime, and violence, and I didn't want to veer off again into that destructive path. Something inside told me I had found the solution to my life's search for purpose, healing, and restoration. I knew, deep in the recesses of my soul, that I needed supernatural help to crawl out of this pit, to redefine what was "normal" for myself and my family, and to literally change my thinking processes.

At night I would go over and over my life, rehearsing how I could have done something different with my life or made better choices. I thought about my baby girl, Mindy, who was being cared for by Billy's mom. Mary lived forty minutes away but didn't like to travel in Indianapolis. She didn't like to go far out of the sphere of her comfort zone. This meant I didn't get to see Mindy very often, and that caused me great grief and pain. Later, Billy was moved to a prison much closer to Mary, which was wonderful. She visited him there often, bringing Mindy along. I was so thrilled Billy could see her and Mindy could have that heart connection at least to her daddy. I still ached for her every single day and by the end of my prison sentence had only been able to see her about ten times.

Jeff, the man who had given Billy the job and invited us to his church, and his parents, Sandy and Harlan, came to visit me every single weekend that I was locked up. I believe they saw it as an investment, a spreading of God's kingdom. They encouraged me so much that it took a bit of the sting away from not seeing Mindy so often. I was so thankful for their mentoring, prayers, and inspiration and the hope they deposited in me with each trip.

Billy wrote to me every single day I was in prison, and I wrote to him Monday through Friday, knowing that these short lines kept us connected—a deep bond that couldn't be broken. I cherished these letters from him and read the lines over and over, holding his words of love close to my heart. Billy somehow finagled his prison into calling my prison so we could talk a couple of times. I'm not sure how he sweet-talked his way into that unheard of happening. Now I realize God was performing miracles all along our path to show us He was real and with us. We also discovered three way calling. This was a new thing back then. We only did this a few times with his mom Mary and Sandy, they both were already doing so much for us. I cherished those moments knowing we would always find a way to each other, no matter how brief.

Stop Wasting Your Paper

Every six months, while in prison, we submitted sentence modifications. These were papers filled out in hopes of getting released early. Since Billy and I had been charged, tried, and sentenced together, all the paperwork came to me. I filled it out three separate times, and they all came back as denied. I was doing my job well in every single position they assigned me, and I stayed out of trouble. I was a model inmate in a minimum-security prison. The first year I kept the faith, read my Bible, stayed in the Word, and steered clear of anything inappropriate or unethical. When we were denied the third time, I was so devastated I gave up and in doing so gave up on God. I wanted out of this prison and wanted my baby back; I wanted to be reunited with Billy. I had believed with everything I had that we would be released early for good behavior, for doing everything the right way.

I knew in my heart we were being made an example of and being punished for my long record of juvenile offenses. It seemed an unfair assessment of people who were trying to make an honest change, and for our first conviction as adults.

The final blow came when I talked to my lawyer, and he had heard through the judge that I shouldn't waste my time filling out another set of sentence modification papers. He told me the judge said not to waste the ink or paper it was written on: "You will do all of your time!" I was crushed, grasping then that I would serve out the rest of my sentence and not be released one second sooner. I had thirteen more months to serve. In Indiana at that time, you did half of your sentence. We had already spent almost two years in prison, away from each other, away from Mindy.

The first year I was in prison I faithfully read the Bible and attended church in prison. After a year passed by and God had not released us early to be with our daughter, I was done with Him. That anger from a life of neglect and abuse that had festered and erupted in various ways, through fighting, violence, drugs, alcohol, partying, and self-contempt, bubbled back up to the surface. I obstinately turned my back and attended church inside the prison only occasionally and let everything I had believed and found hope in fall away bit by bit. I grew cold, hard, and bitter. I had put a time limit on God, and that time limit had expired.

More Regret

Because I had given up hope, I allowed things to intrude into my heart I never would have otherwise. Taylor, a new girl, had entered the prison, and we quickly became acquainted and soon became friends, hanging out together all the time. We clicked, and our personalities meshed. It was like we had a kindred spirit, with many similarities in our lives and thinking. Taylor was very masculine and looked pretty much like a guy—and someone I realized I was becoming attracted to. I reasoned with myself: *you have thirteen more months to serve, Jodie, and there's no hope for you getting out early.* I was returning to my old way of logic that said even if you love someone else, if you can't be with them, then "love the one you're with."

This reasoning tore down all my boundaries of logic and ethics, until I was back to my childhood rut of thinking that was so familiar to me and in some indelible, strange way, almost comforting like an old pair of worn shoes. I soon discovered that Taylor was attracted to me as well. I fought the feelings at first, not wanting to succumb to my desires. But what had started out as a close friendship soon turned into a romantic one. We were together in every way we could be— physically, emotionally, and mentally. I knew it was morally wrong, and I continued writing to Billy through the relationship with her, never disclosing to him about this lesbian relationship with Taylor.

But even as I had turned away from God, Billy was still standing in immovable faith, believing. He had been in prison and dealt with the same struggles, day by day, just as I had. It was hard on him as well, but he stayed strong. Billy had been listening to cassette tapes of preachers like Kenneth Copeland and Kenneth Hagin every day. He had connected with a strong, bold Christian man named Slim who had taken Billy under his wing and was mentoring and teaching him about the Lord. When Billy found out we were denied our sentence modification requests, and that the judge said we should stop trying for sentence modification, instead of giving up he began to pray, declaring daily that we were out of prison, with our daughter, and standing on Proverbs 21:1 that said: "The King's heart is in the hand of the Lord...He turns it whichever way He wills." He claimed that over the judge's heart and would not relent in his constant prayers and decrees.

Billy had remained steadfast the entire time, and when things looked bleak he lifted up our situation to the Lord and said, "God, I know things don't look good, but I give this situation to You. I trust You. Amen." He walked around the prison repeating that prayer over and over as tears poured down his face. He told the Lord, "God, I didn't pray to that judge! I prayed to YOU! And You have told me that now I belong to You, I am a new creation, behold, old things have passed away and all things have become new! They have an innocent man in prison!" He was getting more and more solid in His understanding of God's Word and truth, and He took God at His Word and trusted Him 100 percent. During this time, his faith was much stronger than mine, and I am so thankful he never quit praying, standing, and believing.

Light in the Dark

It was truly a startling miracle when the Indiana Court of Appeals ordered that we be given a second hearing. Our judge had given us an aggravated sentence, and she needed to give a detailed explanation of why. Some corrections needed to be made in our case. When I found out we were to have a surprise court date, maybe three weeks after I had started a relationship with Taylor, I was in complete shock. I had let down my guard and given myself over to my loneliness, turning my back on everything. Now there was a chance I would get out of prison earlier than I had thought possible. Hope rushed over me like a fresh breeze. I hadn't wanted to walk down this path, but I let my instincts, my childhood programming, and my generational moral compass take over. I never wanted to lose my faith again. Hope welled up like fresh, living water on a parched, dry soul.

The day of our unexpected court date came, and the night before I packed up my things in hopes that I wouldn't be coming back. I was keeping my thoughts positive, despite the past twenty-three months of being apart from my husband and daughter. Shackled and handcuffed, I awaited a Muncie sheriff's deputy to come and pick me up. When he started driving in a direction that wasn't toward Muncie, I asked him where we were going, and he said to pick up Billy. My heart nearly exploded with expectation and joy. I hadn't seen him in nearly two years, and now I was headed toward him, knowing that in a few minutes I would behold the face I had longed to see for so long. When we arrived, the policeman locked the doors of the car while I sat inside and waited, my heart beating so hard I could hear it pounding in my ears.

An inmate walking by (this too was a minimum-security prison) came over to the car and said, "Are you Jodie?" When I nodded my head, he grinned and ran inside, and I later found out he had recognized me from a picture Billy had. He told Billy the sheriff was there for him, but someone else was also in the car—Jodie. Soon after, there he was, being led outside by the deputy, and when he got in the car our heads leaned into the other like no time had passed, and we kissed hungrily. It had been so long. It felt so right and so incredible to see him and experience his kiss. I also could tell my husband's demeanor was different. His face literally shone with something I couldn't define, and it made him more handsome, more desirable, to me than he had ever been. This was not the same man who went into prison.

My insides recoiled at the thought that I would soon have to tell him about my relationship with Taylor. I felt unimaginable shame. I had attempted to stay strong and true, but the last year had nearly broken me, and to fall into this just weeks before I found we might get out early staggered me. I pushed it from my mind as the deputy drove us to the jail to await our court time in the afternoon. They allowed us to sit next to each other, without handcuffs, as we were so starved for each other's company. After a meal, we were taken to holding cells until court time. We relished simply being in one another's presence—something we would never take for granted again.

I didn't know what to expect, but this new hope captured my heart and grew every time I glanced at my husband. His faith, his confidence, his body language made me feel safe and secure, and I stood in faith with him. Would Billy be let out? Would I be let out? I was praying with everything in me that at least one of us would be released; then Mindy would have one of her parents back. They led us into the courtroom, and Billy was put in front of the judge first. The appeals court had deemed that they'd been too harsh on us with the sentencing for our first offense as adults, and they spoke some legal jargon. At first I had the distinct feeling that we were going back to prison, but then she spoke these words: "The prosecutor and I have been talking, and we have decided to suspend the rest of your sentence." I grew lightheaded with joy and fear in the same moment. I could barely breathe. Billy would be let out, but would I be released?

They led me in front of the judge as Billy sat back down, and I was shaking so much I could barely stand. My record was a mile long, full of youthful missteps and things I wish I could have changed. I knew she could see it all—every charge, every juvenile visit, every time I got in a fight. It was all recorded. I had been in trouble for my entire life, and in that moment, I reconciled myself to going back to prison. I wanted an unshakable faith that would let me believe I deserved more, that I was worthy of not having my record held against me. And although hope had been rekindled, I resolved myself to the worst-case scenario and was preparing myself mentally.

I looked up at the judge falteringly, and she looked steadily back at me. She repeated that I had been in trouble as far back as she could see, and that's why she'd given me the aggravated sentence. But then she said the very same words that had been said to Billy—after reconsideration, I was being released. God had not abandoned me. I was going home. We were free!

My dad was there, along with several other members of our families, and he paid the only thing barring us from leaving: a $50 fine each. He was sick with the stomach flu, but he was there for us like he never had been for me as a child. Billy's mom, Mary, had brought along a camcorder, and we took turns filming each other, saying silly words of love and happiness, and when we finally walked out of the courthouse, we were completely free. As we stepped outside, we took deep, cleansing breaths of the clean, fresh air. The feeling you have when you regain your freedom? Words are not enough to describe the elation.

After my dad took us all out for lunch at a local restaurant, celebrating our release, we went to Billy's mom's house, where Mindy had been living. We snuck into the house so she wouldn't see us coming, Mindy now being three and a half years old. Billy's grandma, Geneva, was there and had her sitting on the counter in the kitchen with her back turned. She turned her head around, and I'll never forget the look on her face as she said "Mommy!" and reached her arms out toward us in joy, her little face lighting up with a huge smile. We closed the circle and held her tightly. We were home.

PRISON PHOTO OF BILLY

PRISON PHOTO OF BILLY AND MINDY

MINDY'S THIRD BIRTHDAY PARTY AT THE PRISON

MINDY AND ME

MY FAVORITE PHOTO'S OF MINDY AND I

ME AND MINDY

MY DAD VISITING ME IN PRISON

CHAPTER 20

From Dope to Hope

It was all so familiar and yet so new. Billy and I had been able to talk off and on throughout the twenty-three months apart and sent love letters on a weekly basis. But now that we were finally together, able to touch each other, it was surreal. One of our friends, Joann, had known we were going to court, and as a step of faith she reserved and paid for two nights in a hotel. She wanted us to have a place to be alone together so we could get reacquainted. We spent a wonderful night alone together, showing each other just how much we missed each other. I wanted Billy to be my forever love, my one and only for the rest of our lives, and he showed me the same in the most tender of ways.

But the specter of my relationship with the woman in prison hung over me, and I knew I had to tell Billy. We were changing our lives; lying and deception had to go. It was nearly ruining the time I was spending with him, eating away at me, pressing me with its undeniability. Yes, I would need to tell him what had happened eventually, but I couldn't just yet.

We went back to Indianapolis and lived with our friends Jeff and Dianna for the first month after being released. Billy went back to work for him, working construction projects. I found a job on a landscaping crew and rode a lawn mower, making the grass at people's homes look beautiful. I really enjoyed doing this type of work. After a month at Jeff and Dianna's, we moved in with Joann and her family. For four weeks we lived in their basement until we could gather enough money to rent an apartment of our own. We were so thankful for these strong Christian friends who helped us out when we needed it most! Our new apartment was a two-bedroom upstairs apartment; nothing fancy, but it was ours. My dad had stored our old furniture in his garage, and Billy's mom had also stored our car. We just had to get insurance and plates. We had a starting point! We were starting over, and nothing would ever be the same again.

That May, Billy and I worked at a concession stand at the Indy 500 for a friend I had met at the lawncare place. It was a fun job and that is when I discovered I was pregnant again. I told Billy, and he grinned from ear to ear. We were both thrilled. I felt that God was blessing us abundantly for following Him and working hard to do the right thing for our lives.

With each decision we made, every small choice that took us in the opposite direction we once walked, we were marking our path, changing it, and strengthening our obedience to God. It was a difficult path to walk after giving into ungodly desires in our previous lifestyle. But it was completely worth it to get our daughter back, as we still didn't have legal custody of her. Billy's mom was still her guardian, but she began to allow us overnight visits with Mindy, and when she was with us, we felt more complete.

Soon we received a letter from the courts granting us our parental rights back with no strings attached. Mindy was coming home to stay! It was difficult for Billy's mom to let go, as she had raised Mindy since she was eleven months old, and now she was three and a half years old. We couldn't express our gratitude enough for this, but she was our daughter and we wanted her with us.

We started attending a small church nearby, and Billy became very involved in it. I will admit there were many moments I didn't want to be there. I struggled mightily within myself and with what the church and God wanted from me, but I kept attending because I wanted to please Billy. It took nearly a year of going for me to finally admit that I enjoyed being there and wanted to attend faithfully. Billy, on the other hand, made it very clear that church was not an option in our new walk with God. It was a matter of obedience and continuing to learn and grow from God's Word. I had not been shown how to follow a God who was good all the time, who wanted to be with me, fellowship with me, and love on me. A God who believed in me and my potential and had guidelines that would bless us, not hurt us. I didn't believe I deserved to be shown a love like that, but slowly He showed me how to accept and receive it and become a part of a new and wonderful world I never knew was possible or available to me.

God embraced me with His patient, gentle, love, and I began to see that this foreign love truly existed—one that was supernatural enough in its power to win over the hardest of hearts. A love that could heal the brokenhearted, set the captive free, and restore all that the devil had stolen from us. There was mercy with the Lord, grace that I still didn't fully understand, and my broken and bleeding heart pursued it with an unquenchable hunger and thirst. It was the most miraculous and mysterious love I had ever known. The shame and guilt that had wrapped me tight all my life was starting to unravel and fall to the ground like old, dirty clothing.

We hummed along in our post-prison happiness, the kind that comes along with freedom and knowing you've done the time—and that everything is going to be okay. Mindy was growing and thriving, and I was soon big and pregnant with our next little bundle. Our son, Jared, was born on February 3, 1992, and we were overcome with happiness and joy. This little boy had a thick head of black hair, with the biggest brown eyes you ever saw. His eyelashes hung down to his cheekbones. We again fell instantly in love. My mom had been able to come and be at his birth. A son, two children. I couldn't believe how blessed I was to be given such a wonderful gift, and as I held him in my arms, I knew that our family was complete. One little boy and one little girl. We welcomed him into our fold with joy. Mindy was so excited to have a baby brother. She wanted to help me do everything for him. It was a sweet time.

Billy was now singing on the worship team, stretching his talents and offering what he could bring to the table. He always had a phenomenal voice. We actually got to know each other in the choir at White's reform school. He was 100 percent reformed from the inside out, surrendered to God in every way. And now this amazing gift of music was being honed and developed by the Lord as well. Even though I was content and happy with our life, I still struggled with the church aspect—the whole scene of going every week and totally walking away from everything we once knew. I was still bitter about how long the prison sentence had been and that I had missed two years of Mindy's babyhood. It was difficult for me to move ahead, even though I was trying.

Courage

After two years of keeping my secret about Taylor to myself, I finally got enough courage to tell Billy about what had happened in prison. One of my earliest childhood coping mechanisms had been to stuff traumatic realities as deep as possible into a numb location in my mind where I could be in total denial of the trauma. I tried to do this with my memory of Taylor, but God wouldn't let me. He was helping me learn to retrieve those memories and face the realities with His help so that I could receive healing. Now that I was in a safe place, this coping tool was no longer needed as it was when I was a child and couldn't escape the traumas.

I was afraid Billy would leave and wouldn't have faulted him for it. I did exactly what I had done my whole life, shoved the affair with the woman in prison deep down inside. I didn't want Billy, or anyone else, to know. I believe this is why I couldn't enjoy church fully; I was guilt-ridden, covered in shame. A year out of prison I rededicated my life to the Lord, but one more year passed before I could gather the courage to tell Billy this plaguing truth. With great trepidation and fear, I awkwardly announced, "Billy, I have something that I need to tell you." He stopped what he was doing and gave me his complete attention. He sat and listened as I poured the whole story out to him. I told him how the first year in prison I had been faithful to God but lost my way the second year when we weren't released. I turned my back on God, and in doing so, allowed a relationship with this woman mere weeks before we were released.

I could see Billy working in his mind over what I'd told him, considering every fact. And my heart began to heal slowly when he told me that he forgave me and that we would go forward with a fresh start from this point. My relief and joy were tangible, and I wondered why I had waited so long, living with this shame and guilt that haunted me. Prison had taken a lot out of us, and we needed to find a way to remain a team, a force, and keep our little family together strong. My love for Billy deepened that day to a level I never knew possible. This truly was not the same man who went into prison. God had done a miracle in Billy Ballenger. I was in awe.

Goodbye for Now, Mom

Around this time my mom, who had been a source of great pain and woundedness in my life, as well as joy, had finally found happiness. Despite everything she had done to me—not being the mom I needed, neglecting me, abusing me, even encouraging me to be paid for sex—I still loved her desperately. Isn't that the design of things? We cling to those who gave us life, longing for our parents' approval and love, whether they were healthy parents or not, despite their failures and flaws. She had met a man named Jesse who gave her much joy. After her failed relationship with Austin, who I believe to be the biggest love of her life, Jesse brought comfort to her. He was attentive and loving and so much fun to be around. My mom had always been animated and fun, and we would often go up on weekends and stay with them. Our kids were so small, but I wanted them to know my mom and see her for who she was—the life of the party, a person who made you laugh out loud. Their house was full of friends who joined together in jovial revelry, and we had fun whenever we went there.

But as it had always been, she was in and out of the hospital with diabetes and congestive heart failure complications, and since we didn't live in the same town, we didn't always find out when she was sick. I received a call at six in the morning July 1,1994, from the hospital, calling to tell me the family needed to come in and say their last goodbyes to mom. I hung up the phone in shock and looked at Billy while numbly relaying the message. Then I proceeded to lose my grip emotionally and freak out. I had such a mental breakdown at this point that the details are hazy, but I know I was screaming and sobbing uncontrollably, and Billy had to shake me into reality. We hauled the kids out of bed to get them ready to go, and while doing so, the phone rang yet again. It was the hospital, and this time they said the words I dreaded the most to hear: "I'm sorry. Your mom has passed away."

Just like that she was gone. In a robotic fashion we got in the car and dropped the kids off at Billy's mom's house and pointed our car toward Fort Wayne. As we made our way there, I gave up all pretense and wailed inconsolably. Every moment with my mom flashed before my eyes like a fast-forward movie, from a tiny child to this fateful day. I could see her bringing me to agonized tears with her words and the beatings she would lash on us, to the exciting moments when she'd wake us at night with a cheeseburger in a sack to fill our hungry bellies. She was horrible and she was wonderful. A mysterious contradiction I would never fully understand. I loved her fiercely. She was gone. She had just celebrated her fifty-first birthday six weeks ago and was finally leaving behind her dark story of abuse, never quite knowing how to share it with the children who were so easily born to her.

When we finally spilled into the hospital several hours later, she had already been removed and taken to the funeral home. Arriving at the funeral home, we were led to a room where Mom lay on a metal gurney. She was naked except for a sheet that covered her entire body. I stood there frozen in grief, not knowing how to respond to something I was never prepared to see. I hadn't even known she was sick, in the hospital, and here I was staring at her lifeless body. Not even one last smile chiding me for whatever issue she thought I needed to hear about from her. Seeing her corpse traumatized me, but I took it in and allowed myself to feel the thrusting pain, knowing it would be one of the last times to see her. We held her funeral several days later, and I said goodbye to her, leaving behind the pain and trauma with her as she was buried in the hard ground. I was so glad she'd been able to relax and find love before she died. She deserved it as much as I did.

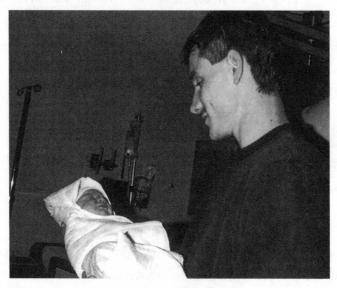

OUR SON JARED'S BIRTH 2/3/92

MOM AND JARED

MY MOM AND HER BOYFRIEND JESSE

CHAPTER 21

Hope Dealers

After several years of helping with various ministries, including Billy singing on the worship team and playing drums, our pastor asked if Billy wanted to lead a church plant on the eastside of Indianapolis only a few blocks from the Women's Prison. Billy jumped at this opportunity, knowing it wouldn't be an easy one. I was raising two small children and wanted to support him in what God was leading him to do. I had my reservations but believed that if God wanted us to do it, we would succeed. It was a small storefront in a not-so-good neighborhood and was called East Michigan Street Word of Faith Family Church. I was now a pastor's wife—not just a prostitute's daughter.

We persevered with the little storefront church we were tending. The rundown building, dirty and in need of care, had a hundred-year-old ceiling, and our church gave us used carpet to put in, which was a blessing because it was a lot better than what was there. Our flock was small, mostly consisting of people who had been diagnosed with mental illness and needed meds, the forgotten ones of society. The rejected and discarded ones. We had little kids who were bringing their toddler brothers and sisters. My heart went out to those kids—some had no shoes—whose parents let them run the streets at night, as well as others who came in off the street and found us. Fights broke out outside our building regularly. Once there was a lady walking down the street with her young son when a van of three women pulled over and started beating the mother. Her son, about seven or eight years old, could do nothing except watch and scream at them to stop. We heard the commotion and ran outside and stopped them. The three women got in their van and drove off. We were able to minister to the lady and her son.

One of the first nights we were there, Billy was leaving the church with a deaf man he was taking home after the service. They had just gotten in the car when they heard a very loud pop. Billy said even the deaf guy jumped, ducked down, and covered his head. Billy looked across the street and saw a guy shooting at another guy. It was almost surreal to find ourselves on the flipside of this life we saw these people living. We were no longer a part of that life, but God now had us throwing out a lifeline to those who were. We did our best, showing love and providing messages to the ones that came and needed hope and deliverance. It was a good place to cut our teeth in ministry, if you will. We held outreaches while we pastored this church, doing gatherings for the community in the parking lot of the public school across the street from us with food, relevant music, and fun, hoping to draw people together and show them God's love.

Billy continued to work construction while we pastored this church, and I focused on raising our two children. After two years, Billy felt strongly that we needed to close the church, believing God had another assignment for us. One night he rented a motel room to get away alone and pray about the decision. He left the room confident it was the right thing to do, and we closed the little storefront church.

We began speaking and sharing our story at various places during this time, knowing we had a miraculous story to tell. For me, everything I had ever been through in my life propelled me to the path I was now on. It needed to be shared. We started attending another church called Spirit of Life Church on the westside of Indy, where Billy sang and played with the praise band, becoming the worship leader after a year and a half. It was at this church that a group of African American ladies loved on me and my family and the healing that brought me from the racial things that had been said and done to me when I was a child was immeasurable. I cherish their friendships. We became certified instructors with Prison Fellowship and participated in this ministry for nearly five years, traveling throughout Indiana and to Kentucky, Arkansas, Mississippi, and Oklahoma to hold seminars in prisons. Billy ministered in high- and low-security prisons for both men and women, and juvenile facilities as well. Through Bill Ballenger Ministries, we shared the testimony of our lives and our time in prison.

Do you remember the man Mrs. Rose spoke of? The one who had high integrity, and if he thought he was misleading you, or told you a lie, he would call himself out and correct it? This was now exactly who my husband had become. Billy was everything I admired about the man she went to school with. I was enamored to be married to someone so honest, so authentic, and with such great integrity. He was showing me through his actions, his day-to-day living, how to be a better person, as well as a Christian.

By the late 1990s, Billy sensed God leading him to record an album of songs. I had watched him become more and more confident in his singing abilities, and he gave me goosebumps when he sang with all he had. Several days before the 9/11 attacks, he recorded his first album in Nashville called *Free at Last*. In January of the following year, we made the decision to go into full-time ministry without holding a secular job as the main source of our income. In that first year, we went to twenty-nine prisons and led twenty-six services at various churches. We recorded another album the next year, and Billy appeared on the TBN Network on the *Praise the Lord* program. This was a special program from Hendersonville, Tennessee, because it was going to be the first show that was aired in China with Paul Crouch, Jeff Fenholt, Lee University Choir, Phil Driscoll, Mark Chironna, and Billy Ballenger. Our mission began to flourish.

Curveballs

But life throws you curveballs, and you either lean into the pitch or let it hit you. In September 2004, our daughter Mindy was now sixteen, and we started to have some issues with her behavior—at least the behavior we demanded of her. We wanted to nip it in the bud before it blossomed. She was seeing a boy, on the sly, that we did not approve of. We had a bad feeling about it, no peace at all, and did everything we could to keep her away from him. Had our upbringing and past destructive choices come into play when it was obvious Mindy was going to fall into some of the same traps and cycles, we had? I know that it did, and we didn't want the same things for her. She refused to stay away from this boy, just as Billy and I refused to stay away from one another, and we became very concerned about the situation. It was enough so that we made the very hard decision to put her into a female Christian boarding school in Missouri. Not only did she insist on seeing this boy, but she was lying to us, manipulating us, running away, and rebelling in every area. Was it the right decision? At the time, we felt that it was, as it temporarily removed her out of a bad situation that was heading for certain catastrophe.

Billy was traveling and making a lot of appearances during this time, and while I went along as often as possible, I also stayed behind frequently to raise Jared, who was quickly growing up. We made the decision in 2005 to move to Branson, Missouri, to be closer to Mindy's boarding school, which was two hours away. We lived there for one year. Mindy was released from the boarding school a month before she turned eighteen. As soon as she turned eighteen and was away from the boarding school, she promptly ran off and hooked up with the same boyfriend. She no longer wanted to live with us, and she married him one year later. Life moves us forward, and we moved forward also the best we knew how.

CHAPTER 22

Break the Grey

Billy had recorded several different albums, including a Christmas album, which opened many doors to Christmas concerts in various locations and churches. He also recorded an original album, with his own songs written and recorded. We knew that God had big plans for us, and we believed in them with all our hearts. Was I ever uncertain about our future? There were times of doubt, I'll admit to that, but I was learning to let go of them and hand them over to God to do with what He would.

During this time Billy felt a deep, driving desire to share our story and music in the public-school system. He knew it was an idea sent straight from God. One day while driving from out of state back to our home in Branson, he believed he heard the Lord say, "Take your story to the public schools, invite them back, and they will come!" And did they ever come! In 2005 Billy began speaking in school assemblies. The authentic way in which Billy spoke captivated students while the message sunk deep into their hearts. Over the years we have seen multiple students impacted in the schools and thousands attend our concert events after school hours. Those that attend our events are met with a relevant musical experience with all the bells and whistles of a major concert performance. At the end of each concert Billy shares what changed his life and saved his family, Jesus Christ. We were called "Teen Rock" in the very beginning as we began touring schools and sharing our story. It was the birth, of what several years later, would be called "Break the Grey". We had finally arrived and felt purpose in what we were doing. It was part of the calling we had been waiting for.

We made several more moves during this time of growing and expanding our ministry, including another stint in Branson as youth directors for a ministry. We ultimately moved to Fort Wayne, Indiana, where our headquarters for Break the Grey resides. But before we settled there, we started using interns from the ministry we were working with to travel with us, performing skits, setting up our assembly equipment, and manning our merchandise table, but we became too busy for their interns to be able to travel with us.

We began to pray about our own internship, as the skits were integral to the entire performance and brought a needed energy and relevance that drew high school and middle school students into the assembly. We made the leap to start our own internship program, incorporating the interns into our organization. In the beginning, they stayed with us at our three-bedroom condo on Morse Lake in Noblesville, Indiana. Everyone squeezed together to make it work; Billy, myself, Jared, and five interns. We scoured northern Indiana looking for the perfect place that is now our Break the Grey headquarters, where our interns stay when not traveling on the road. Having interns, whom we love, adds to our performance tremendously; they're an integral part of the ministry. What began as a three-month internship transitioned to a nine-month internship, August through May. We have first-, second-, and third-year interns. We also added staff members as the ministry grew: director of operations, human resources director, director of internship, and field managers.

Our director of internship oversees our internship program and trains our interns on speaking and performing. The interns are also taught many other skills they will use in their relationships and careers. We have a graduation ceremony and banquet for our graduating interns every May. The internship program has turned into an education for ministry, as well as a discipleship program, that benefits students wanting to be a part of the nitty-gritty of a ministry. Our main Break the Grey offices, where we all work during the day when not traveling, are located one mile away from the intern headquarters and a couple of miles from the church we now attend after resettling in Fort Wayne, Life Bridge Church.

We travel extensively, and I go on most of the trips as well, bringing a message of character development and hope to the many students who are languishing in our school systems. There are so many great school districts, as well as many that are leaving kids behind. I believe our focus on students, especially for me, stems from the hardships faced while growing up. Kids need hope, and if you can get down to their level—really see them and interact in their culture—you can change their lives.

We use a multimedia approach, integrating screens, videos, current music, dance, skits, humor, and motivational speaking, to address the current issues facing youth today: suicide, self-harm, bullying, substance abuse, domestic violence, dating violence, depression, hopelessness, and family dysfunction, among others. We help the kids learn to have dreams and visions for their future, be a part of the change in their schools, respect and honor everyone, and ultimately leave them with HOPE for their futures and achieving their dreams.

We have seen lives saved that would otherwise now be gone. Testimonies pour in of students who decided not to commit suicide, stopped their substance abuse, or stopped dealing drugs. Many of these stories are now included in a testimony book we have put together. We've reached over 320,000 students in the fourteen years Break the Grey has been traveling around the country and Canada. We hope to see that number continue to climb.

Our daughter Mindy is married to Paul, and they have three handsome boys, Chris, Dallas, and Paul Jr. Jared is married as well to his wife, Lauren, and they have a son, Liam, and a daughter, Rigley, our youngest grandchild. My grandchildren are the light of my life and being there for them is one of the biggest pleasures of my life. Billy and I live a busy life, full of wonderful things—things I once never thought it possible to have.

A few years before my mom passed away, she rededicated her life to Jesus. A few days after she passed away Billy had a dream in which she told him that she made it to heaven. My stepmom died of diabetes complications when I was in my early thirties. My dad and I had a DNA test done in December 2018, and it showed a 99.993 percent that he is my biological father. He is married to Shirley, a very nice lady, I have forgiven my dad for not being there for me when I was growing up, I love him very much. I finally found Austin after sixteen years of no communication. He is remarried and happy. Abby, Danny Lee's sister, is now a teacher and happily married. Samantha, Danny Lee's mom, does not live far from Abby and is a caretaker to several of her grandchildren. In June 2017 I found my friend Shelly from middle school. She works in schools as well. We have gotten together a couple of times to catch up with each other. Billy's mom died over twenty years ago at age fifty-two on our son's fourth birthday, and his dad died several years back, in his late sixties. September 2019, I met a brother on my dad's side that had been given to a Catholic agency at birth fifty-eight years ago, he was adopted before he turned one and was adopted by good parents. I am excited to get to know him and his family. Our organization is growing organically into more than we ever imagined, and it keeps us busy running it. We are on the road almost constantly, and it is a beautiful thing that brings us great joy.

The start of my life, though rocky, did hold moments and memories I will forever treasure. Along with those painful memories that cling to me stubbornly, I can see my mom now through the lens of many years of experience and events of my own, simply struggling to be a mom. She brought much baggage with her to the job and was never able to put that baggage down. What I learned through coming into a relationship with Jesus Christ and His Word was that it didn't define who I was—Jodie.

God has a plan for each of our lives, and potential and purpose lay in each one of our hearts. Our pasts don't have to define or control us. Before my personal relationship with Jesus, I was a broken person, but through Jesus I have been healed of past wounds, set free from the bondage of generations of ungodly thought patterns. We each can go as far and as fast with the Lord as we are willing to go by stepping out in faith. I made choices that reflected what I had been shown and taught, but I didn't need to wear that heavy coat of shame for the rest of my life. I've lain it down at Jesus' feet and picked myself up. The little girl who did drugs, was sexually abused and promiscuous, and grew into a teenager who went to prison for poor choices is only a part of who I once was. That person is no longer who I am. I am now free from any condemning labels, as they no longer stick to me. I am me, Jodie, defined only by who God says I am: His child.

I am Beautifully UNBROKEN.

Beautifully Unbroken

A Quick-Start Guide to Help You Heal

The Bible is full of stories of women whose lives were touched, changed, and completely turned upside down by the power of God. And many women throughout the course of history, just like Jodie, have their own personal stories of how God came into their life, transformed their heart, and set them on a new path of life in Him. God wants to do a powerful work in your life too!

All of us have experienced the pain of brokenness. Whether caused by our selves or others, brokenness left unhealed can affect so many areas of our lives. Brokenness can result from many things, including but not limited to physical, emotional, and spiritual abuse. Jodie experienced incredibly deep brokenness on many levels throughout her life, and now God has given her a voice to carry the truth of His healing and redemptive power to others who are broken and in need of a true, lasting healing.

This study will revisit many of the areas of brokenness Jodie shared throughout her story and equip you with the power and strength to face your brokenness so you too can find freedom, forgiveness, and a healing that will mend you into the Beautifully Unbroken person you were always created to be.

New Life in Christ

Jesus came to earth to save us from our sin and to redeem and restore our brokenness. He is the only One who can create something beautiful out of our personal pain and struggles and set us free to live a new life in Him. The rest of this study will be meaningless if the most important part of Jodie's story isn't shared first—her relationship with God.

Romans 3:23 – For all have sinned and fall short of the glory of God.

What does this mean? And what is sin? Romans 3:23 is a scripture in the Bible that tells us "all"—meaning every single human being who has or ever will exist on the face of this earth—has sinned against God. Sin, simply put, is disobedience to God and how He wants us to live our lives. A few examples of sin are lying, selfishness, hatred, lust, and putting anything above God in your life. Those are just a few of the many things considered sin. Guilty? Yeah, you're not alone! We all are.

Romans 6:23 – The wages of sin is death; but the gift of God is eternal life through Christ Jesus our Lord.

John 3:16 – For God so loved the world that He gave His only begotten Son, that whoever believes in Him should not perish but have everlasting life.

The penalty for our sin is death, and that death is an eternal separation from God. Jesus, God's Son, came to earth over two thousand years ago and died in your place so that you wouldn't have to pay the penalty for your sin.

Romans 10:9 – If you confess with your mouth the Lord Jesus and believe in your heart that God raised Him from the dead, you will be saved.

The Bible tells us that salvation is a gift from God. But what is He saving you from? Your sin and a life apart from Him! All you have to do is accept this gift. There is nothing you can do to earn it; it's already been paid for!

Prayer for a New Life with God

If you are ready to begin a new life with God, you can pray this prayer to God, or pray your own words:

God, I am ready to begin a new life in you. I want You to save me from my sin and from a life apart from You. I invite You to come into my life, change me, transform me, and set me on a new path with You. I ask You to help me live my life and to know You more. In Jesus' name, AMEN!

Equip Yourself for Your New Life

A few tips to equip you to live a new life with God:

Buy yourself a Bible and read it. The Bible is God's love letter and instruction book for life written just for you! It can be hard to know where to start, so try starting in the book of John. God desires for you to know Him, and reading the Bible is a great way to get to know God.

Plug into a church that teaches God's truth. Finding a church that you can plug into is vital for your new journey. Many churches not only have services on Sunday mornings but also have separate Bible study classes or small groups you can get connected to.

Pray for and find a godly mentor. Having a Christian mentor will help you grow in your faith. They can help answer your questions, encourage you, and keep you accountable.

Pray to God regularly. Prayer is simply communicating with the God of the universe, the One who created you and loves you more than you can comprehend! You don't have to use fancy words or pray a certain way. You can do this in your bedroom, in your car, in the shower—anywhere!

Loss

Jodie, like many of us, has experienced deep and devastating losses throughout her life. Some of her losses include the death of her first love, Danny, to a tragic automobile accident; abandonment by her father and mother; homelessness; betrayal from friends; losing custody of her daughter for two years and her freedom through imprisonment; her mother's eventual death; and even her relationship with Billy for a short period of time. Whether by death or by choice, experiencing a loss can leave long-lasting wounds in our minds and scars on our hearts.

What losses have you faced in life?

Some examples: death of a loved one, divorce, an estranged relationship, betrayal, losing your job, losing your home, etc.

Scripture:

Philippians 4:19 – And my God shall supply all your need according to His riches in glory by Christ Jesus.

Prayer:

God, I pray that You would heal areas of my heart and mind that have been wounded from loss in my life. I ask that You restore me through Your presence, joy, and love and remind me that I have everything I need in You. In Jesus' name, AMEN!

Commitment

Commitment is something we all want and even expect in life, whether it's from our parents, a significant other, an employer, or a friend. Broken commitments from many loved ones throughout her life left Jodie with a crippling inability to both expect commitment from others and also to be a committed person herself, especially when it came to relationships. When Jodie and Billy began dating, Jodie never expected Billy to stick around, but he did! He went to great lengths to see the one he loved, doing anything he had to do just to be with her. True commitment goes beyond your feelings, emotions, and even circumstances, resolving yourself to "stick it out," whether it's a relationship, a job or task, or something as simple as keeping your word. God is faithful, and He will always remain committed to you.

Has lack of commitment left areas of brokenness in your life?

Some examples: failed relationships, neglectful parents, abandoned friendships, broken promises, etc.

Scripture:

Psalm 37:5 – Commit your way to the Lord, Trust also in Him, and He shall bring it to pass.

Philippians 1:6 – Being confident of this very thing, that He who has begun a good work in you will complete it until the day of Jesus Christ.

Prayer:

God, I thank You that You are a committed God, and I pray that You would help me to be a committed follower of You. I thank You that even if I've never experienced true commitment from anyone on earth, You will always be committed to me. Help me to be a person of my word and to allow You to continue working in my life. In Jesus' name, AMEN!

Rejection, Abandonment, and Feeling Alone

Rejection stings painfully and leaves a lasting poison that can affect so many areas of your life, including your self-esteem, how you treat others, and how you view life. Jodie faced rejection from kids at school and church and from her dad, mom, uncle, and stepmom, just to name a few. Abandoned by her mom and dad many times, she lived a life woven with threads of feeling alone and unwanted. This caused her to put up a wall and become a hardened person, even though on the inside all she really wanted was to feel and know what it means to be truly wanted, accepted, and loved unconditionally.

Have you experienced rejection, abandonment, or feeling alone in life?

Some examples: a broken relationship, being excluded from a group, employment rejection, going after a dream only to have it fail, etc.

Scripture:

Hebrews 13:5 – Let your conduct be without covetousness; be content with such things as you have. For He Himself has said, "I will never leave you nor forsake you."

Jeremiah 31:3 – The Lord has appeared of old to me, saying: "Yes, I have loved you with an everlasting love; Therefore with loving-kindness I have drawn you."

Prayer:

God, help me to know that nothing can ever separate me from Your love. You will never leave me nor forsake me, and You love me with an everlasting love. I pray that You would heal me from the effects of rejection and abandonment in my life and help me to love myself and others as You do. In Jesus' name, AMEN!

Regret and Repentance

Regret. Does reading that word trigger memories you wish you could erase? Repentance means sincere regret or remorse. Jodie's life was filled with drug abuse, promiscuity, violence, and a plethora of unwise choices. While she will never be able to erase the mistakes of her past, she has chosen to allow God to forgive her of her past and give her a new future. God has given us many promises in the Bible, along with the power and ability to move on from our old lives and begin anew in Him!

What regrets do you carry that you need to give to God and leave in the past?

Scripture:

Romans 2:4 – The kindness of God leads you to repentance.

Psalm 103:12 –As far as the east is from the west, So far has He removed our transgressions from us.

Romans 8:1 – There is therefore now no condemnation to those who are in Christ Jesus, who do not walk according to the flesh, but according to the Spirit.

Philippians 3:13-14 – Brethren, I do not count myself to have apprehended: but one thing I do, forgetting those things which are behind and reaching forward to those things which are ahead, I press toward the goal for the prize of the upward call of God in Christ Jesus.

Prayer:

God, I thank You that my past is no longer who I am and that You have given me the power and ability to leave it behind me. You have given me a new life in You. I pray that You will heal me from the effects of my past. Heal my mind, my body, and every single part of me that needs Your touch. I ask that You help me know who I am as a Christian. In Jesus' name, AMEN!

Betrayal

Betrayal is deeply devastating and heartbreaking, especially when it's caused by someone you love. Jodie experienced painful betrayal on many levels—in her marriage, from her family, and from friends. Billy's mom even betrayed them by stealing money and falsely reporting them to CPA. Betrayal can cut you to the core and leave you with an unwanted inability to trust and love again.

Have you experienced betrayal or betrayed others?

Some examples: infidelity, broken confidence in a relationship, gossip, lies, etc.

Scripture:

Proverbs 11:13 – A talebearer(gossiper) reveals secrets, But he who is of a faithful spirit conceals a matter.

Psalm 89:33 – Nevertheless my loving kindness I will not utterly take from him, nor allow my faithfulness to fail.

Prayer:

God, I pray that You would heal my heart and mind from any betrayal that has happened to me, and I pray for forgiveness for times I may have betrayed others. Help me to know and believe that You are always faithful and will never betray me. I want to trust You with my entire life. In Jesus' name, AMEN!

Devastation, Destruction, and Disappointment

How do you feel when your plans and expectations don't meet reality? Like Jodie, when this becomes common in our life, we often stop hoping for anything better and view life through faulty, pessimistic lenses. Maybe we really do want to hope for the best, but we often end up expecting the worst in the back of our minds. Jodie was conditioned to think and expect certain things in life because of her upbringing; it was all she knew, so that's how she functioned. She expected relationships to end, lies to be acceptable, and manipulation to be a means to an end. Devastation from frequent let-downs, coupled with destruction leaving its mark on many areas of her life, left a large platform for disappointment in Jodie's life. The kingdom of God doesn't operate by devastation, destruction, and disappointment, but rather by truth and love.

Have you experienced devastation, destruction, and disappointment in life?

Scripture:

Jeremiah 29:11 – For I know the thoughts that I think toward you, says the Lord, thoughts of peace and not of evil, to give you a future and a hope.

Romans 12:12 –rejoicing in hope, patient in tribulation, continuing steadfastly in prayer

Psalm 103:2-4 – Bless the Lord, O my soul, and forget not all His benefits: Who forgives all your iniquities [sins], Who heals all your diseases, Who redeems your life from destruction, Who crowns you with lovingkindness and tender mercies.

Prayer:

God, thank You that You have a plan and purpose for my life, and I pray that You would help me to view life through Your eyes instead of faulty lenses. Renew my mind with truth and love, in Jesus' name, AMEN!

Determination

Jodie was created with a strong, determined personality. Nothing can stop the plans of a determined person who has their mind made up. Once Jodie laid eyes on Billy, she was set on winning his heart, and nothing—including the other girls pining for his affections—was going to stop her. After being released from prison, Billy and Jodie were determined to use their story to reach and impact the lives of others, and they have not let anything come in the way of making this a reality.

What dreams or aspirations do you have? What is something you want the determination to see through? What are some ways you can share God's love with others or use your story to make an impact?

Scripture:

Philippians 4:13 – I can do all things through Christ who strengthens me.

Prayer:

God, thank You for giving me the strength to do all things. Your love is powerful, and it compels me to want to live a determined life with You. God, help me to stay strong in my faith and to allow You to show me the ways You want to use me to impact this world. In Jesus' name, AMEN!

Compromise

One definition of compromise is "to accept a standard lower than what is desirable." Compromise can cause us to do things for a moment that we will regret for a lifetime. This could happen in a relationship, a job, school, friendships, and countless other areas of life. Jodie and her friends compromised their purity when a young man seduced each of them individually while hanging out. Peer pressure is often a gate for compromise, persuading us to do things we would never think of doing otherwise. Allowing the Word of God to dictate our behavior and lifestyle will help to keep us on a good path and avoid times of compromise.

Have you compromised in areas of your life?

Scripture:

Romans 13:14 – But put on the Lord Jesus Christ, and make no provision for the flesh, to fulfill its lusts.

2 Corinthians 5:17 – Therefore, if anyone is in Christ, he is a new creation: old things have passed away; behold, all things have become new.

Philippians 1:27 –(first part)-Only let your conduct be worthy of the gospel of Christ

Prayer:

God, I thank You that my past compromises don't have to be a part of who I am anymore. I am a new creation in You. I pray forgiveness over my past and ask You to help me have a new future without compromise. Help me to live the life You want me to live. In Jesus' name, AMEN!

Choices

Life is full of choices. From the moment we open our eyes in the morning to the moment we shut them at night, we are constantly bombarded with choices. Some are seemingly insignificant, while others can be life-changing. Jodie's life, up until she came to God, was a revolving door of bad choices—drugs, alcohol, and bad relationships, to name a few. Someone cared enough to share about Jesus with Jodie, and she chose to turn away from her old life and embrace a new life with Him. Because of her choice to follow God, her life has never been the same since!

What life choices have you made for the good and for the bad?

Scripture:

Joshua 24:15 – ...Choose for yourselves this day whom you will serve.... But as for me and my household, we will serve the Lord.

1 John 5:12 – He who has the Son has life; he who does not have the Son of God does not have life.

John 3:15 – that whoever believes in Him should not perish but have eternal life.

Psalm 146:2 – I will praise the Lord all my life; I will sing praise to my God as long as I live.

Prayer:

God, thank You that You have given me the freedom of choice. Today, Lord, I choose to follow You. I want to know You more and live my life in a way that honors You. Help me to do this now and forever, in Jesus' name, AMEN!

KNOW WHO YOU ARE IN CHRIST: Read Ephesians entire book, Romans chapter 8, 2 Corinthians chapter 5, Genesis chapters 1-3.

Stay in touch with us @ Jodieballenger.com, Breakthegrey.com, Billyballenger.com

Please consider sharing and reviewing my book on social media and with friends.

Do you have an outreach to jails, prisons, juvenile centers, etc.? Please consider using my book as a reference of how Jesus changes lives.

BILLY AND MINDY AFTER A SCHOOL ASSEMBLY

BILLY IN CONCERT

OUR CLOSE FRIENDS AND THE COUPLE THAT WITNESSED TO US

JEFF & DIANNA CLAMPITT

MINDY AND HER FAMILY PAUL CHRIS PJ & DALLAS

JARED AND HIS FAMILY LAUREN LIAM RIGLEY

BEAUTIFULLY UNBROKEN

BEFORE THE WEDDING

OUR 26TH WEDDING ANNIVERSARY

THE WEDDING WE ALWAYS WANTED

CHOREOGRAPHED DANCE WITH OUR WEDDING PARTY AND

BREAK THE GREY INTERNS AND STAFF

Resources

www.remedylive.com
24/7 Texting
Text REMEDY to 494949 to chat about
abuse, anxiety, bullying, depression, drugs and alcohol, eating
disorders, faith, pornography,
self-harm, suicide

Suicide Prevention
Call 1-800-273-TALK (8255)

Crisis Text Line
Text HOME to 741741
www.crisistextline.org

Aspire
24-Hour Crisis Line
1-800-560-4038

<u>Sex Trafficking</u>
Are you being forced to do anything you do not want to do?
Have you been threatened if you try to leave? Have you wit-
nessed young girls being prostituted? If so, please call the
National Human Trafficking Hotline
(24/7) at 1-888-373-7888

www.TraffickFree.com

Educate yourself about sex trafficking and sexually exploited children in the US and learn about the red flags of trafficking and how to identify a victim. This organization is run by Theresa Flores, a human trafficking survivor who wrote about her experience in the book *The Slave Across the Street*, a *USA Today* and *Wall Street Journal* bestseller.

More Books . . .

Not for Sale: The Return of the Global Slave Trade – and How We Can Fight It
Stolen: The True Story of a Sex Trafficking Survivor
In Our Backyard: Human Trafficking in America, and What We Can Do to Stop It
Renting Lacy: A Story of America's Prostituted Children (A Call to Action)

See a list of behaviors of a pimp/trafficker and warning signs that an individual is being trafficked, how to report it, and more resources at
www.sharedhope.org/join-the-cause/report-trafficking